Create An Impact

Achieving peace inside, results outside

Jeet Kumar

Published by Abundant Coaching

www.abundantcoach.com

Cover by Jennifer Barker

ISBN: 9-798-44786-355-5

To all the people who want to create an impact and make a difference on this planet.

Table of Contents

"Believe it can be done. When you believe something can be done,
really believe, your mind will find the ways to do it. Believing a
solution paves the way to solution." — David J. Schwartz

Acknowledgments

"The roots of all goodness lie in the soil of appreciation for all goodness" — Dalai Lama

For the creation of this book, I owe many thanks to...

My wife, Vijju: Thank you for being there for me in both the good times and the challenging times. You are my pillar in life. I have moved you from continent to continent and city to city, and you have always shown up and supported me for what I wanted to create on this planet. Without you, it would have been extremely difficult, if not impossible, for me to be who I am today. You play so many roles in my life. Most importantly, you are my best friend with whom I share so many good things. Because of you, my life is possible.

My kids, Jai and Jiya: When I look at both of you, you give me peace and comfort in knowing that I don't ever need to worry about either of you. You have both become extremely responsible at such a young age. Because you two are the way that you are, it allows me to do what I do. Had you not become responsible human beings, I would always be concerned and worried about you and would not have been able to create this.

The dad that I always miss. Dad, though I don't have any memories of spending time with you because I lost you at such a young age, you have always been with me. Thank you for being the unseen source of power, guidance, inspiration.

The happy memory of my mother: Mom, although you are not with me, what we went through during my early nesting stages of life shaped me, colored me, and helped put me on the path of who I am today. You made a tremendous contribution by bringing me on this planet.

My four sisters: You all were there for me when I needed you the most and you all helped shape my life. Thank you for all of your love and support as I was growing up. Thank you for sharing your life with me and being such an important part of my life story.

My extended family and childhood friends: Throughout this book, I share many stories about the times when I was growing up. When I look back on these times, you all made my initial days less painful. You being there made a difference in my life.

My business partners, Dan, Sandeep, Matt, Rakesh: We all came from different places and different cultures and yet we still came together for one shared vision of creating abundance on this planet. You are all less of business partners to me, and more of my brothers. My life is much more meaningful and fulfilled because you are on this journey with me.

All of the employees at In Time Tec: Thank you for your unshakable stand for creating abundance. Thank you for trusting me as your leader and making this platform possible. Your hard work and dedication to loving every human being and being your best self are inspiring.

All of the individuals whose stories are featured in this book: Thank you for sharing your stories, as this book would have not otherwise been possible. I appreciate you trusting me with your life and letting me be a part of your transformation.

The communication team at In Time Tec: Thank you for coming along with me to make many things possible, including this book. You help me share my passion for this platform and creating abundance, both inside and outside of this company. Thank you for being my partners in this creation.

To the domain experts who worked behind the scenes to help create this book, I deeply appreciate your contribution: Stacy Ennis, Cienna Madrid, and Chantel Fox.

Thank you to all of the people who have spent countless hours reading this book and providing feed-forward. Your commitment to making a difference in the lives of readers has created an impact.

Here's to many more years of creating an impact on this planet.

I love you all so much!

Evidence of Success: An Introduction to the Power of This Work

I first met Jeet during a Skype meeting in January of 2009. I was still working at HP and had recently chosen to join a group of founders to create a new company, In Time Tec. My initial impressions of Jeet were that he was an intelligent, caring, thoughtful, and resourceful human being. While all true, at least to me, I also completely underestimated him. What I missed that day, and truthfully for several years following our initial interaction, was the kind of leader he was and the immense amount of hard work he had done and was continuing to do to grow his leadership capabilities. You see, for Jeet, leadership is a mountain with no top. If being a leader is what you are up to in life, you need to enjoy climbing because the journey never ends. I didn't realize it yet, but for me, that fateful day in January was the start of my climb.

I had spent the previous 13 years building my career from a junior software engineer fresh out of college to a senior software engineer, a technical lead, an MBA graduate, and finally joining the management ranks. It was a fast climb, and I was doing it at a young age. I was also doing it the way I had always done it. I was consistently producing results. What I was missing, which was a total blind spot for me, was how I was producing results and the associated cost of production. Undeniably, I was a "my way is the right way" or, even more harshly, "my way is the only way" person. Contributing to my blind spot was that the feedback loop looked good from where I stood. When I did it my way, results were produced, and I was rewarded. Wash. Rinse. Repeat. Do these enough times, and you move up the corporate ladder. The move upwards only reinforces the behavior, and you keep rolling with what appears to be working. However, the problem was I had been missing part of the equation. Results were showing up on the outside, and simultaneously, I had very little peace on the inside.

Thinking back to my cubicle at HP, I had what was typical at the time. An 8ft x 8ft workspace with high gray walls and a 2ft opening. As the years passed, the inside of my workspace changed. Books, computers, monitors, printers, and family pictures came and went with the times. However, as I started to take on more and more responsibility within the organization, one thing became a constant. Always on my desk, somewhere between the keyboard and the monitor, a small bottle of ibuprofen sat there. The bottle did change over time because I regularly needed to replace it. Why? Stress was causing me almost constant tension headaches. The tension headaches were a symptom of my stress. But what was stress symptomatic of? From what I stand now, a transformed human being with a different outlook on leadership and life, I can see it stemmed from a lack of peace on the inside.

My lack of peace on the inside carried with me into my entrepreneurial career at In Time Tec. The work had changed, the people around me had changed, my responsibilities changed, and the lack of peace remained. Things stayed that way until late 2014. My father had recently passed away from Non-Hodgkin's Lymphoma, the work I was doing at the time was incredibly challenging, and I was miserable. My lack of peace was at an all-time high, affecting my relationships with my co-founders and co-workers. In December, Jeet and Dan (another In Time Tec co-founder who you will hear about more in this book) visited me in Oregon for a founder's retreat to Mt. Hood. I picked them up at the airport, and we drove straight up to the mountain to grab lunch at Government Camp. The drive was quiet. Ominous really. There was an elephant in the room, and that elephant was me. My lack of peace wasn't working for people, and it was time for Jeet and Dan to do something about it. I could sense it. The tension in the air was palpable. When we reached the restaurant (I'll never forget the table), I finally opened up. I finally got vulnerable. And I finally shared what was eating me up inside. At that moment, things changed. Don't get me wrong, it's not as if my transformation was immediate. But it unlocked the doors and gave them permission to get involved in my life and help me.

A few months later, in February of 2015, I found myself at the same personal development program Jeet attended in 2007. The next four days profoundly changed my life. I finally started to get access to what was causing my stress and my lack of peace. I could feel the weight lifting from me in that short time, both mentally and physically. Upon returning home to Oregon, my wife Amy picked me up at the airport for a quick lunch date before returning to the office. At lunch, she commented that she could tell I looked lighter, freer, and happier as she was driving up to the curb. She was right. I was.

Since 2015 I've had the blessing of Jeet's direct coaching and leadership, and things for me have only continued to improve, and my life is so much more fulfilling than it was back in 2009. Through his coaching and my own hard work, I've learned what it takes to have peace inside and results outside. From where I stand, this is how to live a life of meaning, purpose, joy, and love. As you continue to read this book, this is the world you are about to enter.

Knowing Jeet is knowing someone who is here to make a difference in this world. Create an Impact takes what Jeet has learned over the years and puts it into a practical framework to help you achieve results and achieve them with the internal peace that is so valuable in today's complex, fast-moving and ever-changing world. Starting with Explore, Jeet takes you on a journey of self-discovery as before you can create, you need to understand who you are and why you do what you do. Once you've explored yourself and have gained a better understanding of self, Jeet takes you to Create, where you uncover being others-focused, love, the powerful nature of language and action, and finally, how to take (and be) a stand for your life and the lives of others. And finally, there is Celebrate, where you learn to appreciate the results of your creation (even when things don't go the way you planned), connect with your greatness, and celebrate life.

After each chapter, there are a series of questions. I'd implore you to take a measured pace through the book. There's no need to rush from chapter to chapter. At the end of each chapter, take your time to do what Jeet describes as "the intellectual work" to thoughtfully answer each question. Write them down. Reflect on them. It's important work because it's not just about you and your life. It's about the lives of those around you. One of my friends says, "you think you're a thermometer when really you're a thermostat." I take this to mean that the ripple effect of your behavior goes beyond just you, whether you realize it or not. Your behaviors don't only measure your temperature, they set the temperature for people in your life.

Be a leader, be peaceful, generate results around you, and create an impact in this world.

Peace and Love,

Matt Fratzke, friend and fellow co-founder of In Time Tec

Foreword

I don't remember exactly when I first met Jeet. I know it was probably around 2009. I think he was with his business partner Dan Puga. But I don't remember the specifics. When I think back on that time, there isn't anything that stands out about our first interactions. But I cannot even begin to explain how much Jeet stands out to me now. In the 10+ years that I have known Jeet, I have watched him not only grow In Time Tec into the successful company it is but also grow himself into a powerful leader and inspiring human.

You will read in these pages about his journey. But what you won't see is the firsthand experience of working with him. You won't see how driven and genuine he is. You won't see how quickly and passionately he takes action. You won't see the level of care and love he has in everything he does. What you will see is how he got to where he is and why his words are impactful.

Jeet's life experiences serve as a foundation for this book. It's admirable how he's turned his life into something that can help other people. Jeet's genuine nature towards life reflects in this book. Everything in these pages is intuitive and comes straight from the heart- because that is who Jeet is!

In life, we tend to overcomplicate things. We overlook our basic needs and lose focus on what we're working towards. This book is all about examining your life and figuring out what you value and how that impacts your choices. It's essential to know what you are creating and how it impacts other people. In this book, Jeet helps us understand how we all have a desire to create positive meaning in our lives.

"Create an Impact" not only covers creation but celebration. Too often, we get so caught up in trying to accomplish something and forget to celebrate what we've created.

This book helps you establish a system for looking at your life and examining what you need. You have the power to enhance your own life, and Jeet's book helps you do that.

I am glad Jeet took his life experiences and turned them into a resource for other people. I have learned a lot from him over the years and I hope "Create an Impact" teaches you some of what Jeet's taught me.

Jay Larsen, President of the Idaho Technology Council

SELF-REFLECTION

What do you want to get out of this book?

_____
_____
_____
_____
_____
_____

Identify one to three areas of your life where you want to make the biggest impact?

_____
_____
_____
_____
_____

In which areas are you not seeing your desired change, progress, or growth?

_____
_____
_____
_____
_____
_____

What results do you want to see in these areas?

_____
_____
_____
_____
_____
_____

From "Why me?" to "Why not me?"

> **"**
>
> *"Understand that one day you will have the power to make a difference. Use it well."* — Mindy Kaling, *"Why Not Me?"*

To say that India gets hot in the summer is like calling the Taj Mahal a nice house: both are vast understatements. Where I come from in India, temperatures in the summer rise to about 120°F/49°C. In many of the smaller villages, as in my native village of Nagar in Rajasthan, there is no respite from the heat except at night when the temperature drops to 79°F/26°C. As you can imagine, this does little to actually cool your body.

And yet, despite the bodily discomfort, we all anticipated summer like a visit from an old friend. The year I turned eight, my family and I spent the day of Ganga Dussehra — a Hindu festival celebrating the end of summer and beginning of fall — on the rooftop watching kites fly. The sky was speckled with so many dizzying colors that the effort of focusing on just one kite caused your eyes to blink and water. Young children and older generations were on other rooftops and down on the ground, battling to have the highest flyer. It was tradition for us to watch the kites during the day, enjoy dinner on the roof of our home at dusk, and then lay our bedsheets out on the roof and sleep there. We did this often, as it was cooler outside of our home than inside.

My uncle's family lived next to us and we shared a rooftop. When the sun started to set, the women in both my house and my uncle's house began bringing food up the stairs from the kitchens to the roof. I was running and jumping from roof to roof, expending my exuberant energy. I noticed that my aunt — the wife of my late-father's brother — had prepared a metal bowl full of delicious mango juice to go with dinner for her family. I desperately wanted some. The smells wafting from the bowl made my mouth water. The condensation running down the sides further proved just how refreshing my glass of juice could be. Being eight and not yet understanding family dynamics and expectations, I asked my aunt if I could have some juice.

"Ask your mother to make you some," she said. "I have only made enough for my little family."

I ran to our side of the roof and pulled on my mom's sari. "Ma! Can we make some mango juice?"

In response to my question, I received a smack upside the head. "Little boys with no fathers do not get mango juice," my mother said.

The smack did not shock me so much as the realization that being fatherless meant I was "less than" others, at least in our culture. Of course, I had grown up keenly aware of my father's emotional and physical absence. I ached for a father. My father passed away when I was still a toddler, leaving my mother with four young daughters and a small boy who would not be able to provide for the family until he was older. You see, men were traditionally the providers of the household, and not having an adult male in my Indian family in the seventies meant that we did not have money for much, and especially not for frivolous things like mangos for juice.

One innocent request for juice was answered with several painful revelations that day:

- I would always be judged harshly by others for not having a father.
- Our poverty was a direct result of his death.

- My family's life would not improve until I was old enough and skilled enough to improve it myself.

As an eight year old, these realizations were overwhelming. It felt weird in the moment. My heart clenched like a fist in my chest. I knew something was wrong, but at that age, I couldn't quite figure out what or recognize the impact of what I had learned. Suddenly, the kites in the sky didn't seem as bright and carefree. Their flight patterns looked frantic, like caged birds fluttering in all directions, searching for an escape.

I broke a little that day. Or perhaps I was just forced to grow up before my time. I spent many years asking the universe, "Why me?" Why couldn't I be like the other boys in my native village? Why did I have to borrow cricket gear and wear hand-me-down clothes? Why did seeing other boys working with their fathers, learning from them, make me hang my head in shame and misery? Why was my life so difficult?

Until I was twenty, I nurtured that attitude of self-pity. Each bump or curveball life threw at me, I would wonder, "Why me?" Or I would think, "Woe is me!" Yet I had this instinctive knowledge that life could be better for me and life could be better for others. Despite this, it took me years to understand the connection between my self-defeatist attitude and my lack of success in life.

That changed in 1992, on the eighteenth anniversary of my father's death. That summer I was living back at home after receiving my diploma from junior college. I had applied to an engineering college in Jaipur and was waiting to see if I got accepted. But getting accepted was only half the battle; I still needed to figure out how to afford tuition if I got in.

I had also received a job offer from a company in Bhiwari, near Delhi, as a supervisor at a factory that manufactured electronic capacitors. That option felt limited, like my contribution in life would be fixed. But it also meant I would immediately earn money to help my family: 500 rupees, or about 15 dollars a month.

I had a choice to make. On this particular June day, it was weighing on me as heavy as the Indian heat. No part of my heart leaped at the chance to work in a factory, likely for the rest of my life. I instinctively knew that life could be better if only I was brave enough to push myself.

Yet I also realized I would have to work harder than others to have the same things they did. However, I finally had hope that if I changed my mindset and took systematic steps to outline my goals and how best to reach them, life could be better for me. It could be better for others. That mantra has stayed in my heart ever since.

From growing up in India, to moving to the United States, to growing a multimillion-dollar global software company, I have learned there are two ways to live. You can live as I did for the first twenty years of my life, as if life happens to you. You don't know why you are here or how to change your circumstances, or if you can at all. Or, you can live life as a celebration. You get to choose why you are here, then decide for yourself what you can accomplish.

Most humans live the first way, not knowing how to give their life meaning or define what their life is about. These people might be content — happy, even — but they feel stuck. They know there are bigger things out there, and they want to be more, do more, and have more. Yet they can't quite figure out *how*. They keep waiting for a sign, or a milestone, or a "someday, one day" that is impossible to reach. They don't realize that the only thing getting in the way is themselves.

If this is you, your sign, milestone, someday, one day is here.

The morning that changed my worldview, and through it my life, I had woken up early to prepare for Sraddha. This is a ritual through which we express our gratitude toward those who have passed on. On the anniversary of their death, we offer food to them through four different channels: fire, water, cow, and crow. My mother and sisters were in our tiny kitchen, elbow to elbow with sweat-drenched brows, preparing the food for the offerings. It is traditional to fast until all the offerings have been accepted. My stomach rumbled as I walked out of the house to get the brahmanaas, the priest who would perform the ceremony.

I navigated the dirt streets of my native village, feeling the sadness of not having a father and the resentment of having to support my family because he was not around. I passed many storefronts on the way to the temple. As I looked at the shopkeepers, I could see the years of hard work, family obligation, and caretaking in the wrinkles and dirt on their faces. I waved hello to my friends and their fathers, their feet sometimes bare and their stores sometimes busy.

I arrived back at my home with the brahmanaas. He led us through prayers and blessings for our father, as we had done every year since my father's death: "Let the ancestors residing on Earth attain an evolved region. Let the ancestors who are in heaven, that is, at a higher plane of existence, never degrade. Let the ones who are at a medium plane of existence attain a higher plane. Let the ancestors who symbolize the Truth protect us."

Then, my mother brought out a plate of food and started a small fire in the homa altar in the middle of our floor. She took a large pinch of the food and set it in the fire. We then offered food to the priest as an appreciation for conducting the ceremony. From there, I visited a nearby well and dropped some food into the water. I stopped to offer more to a cow, which is a sacred creature to Hindus. The final part of the ritual was to set the remaining food on our rooftop for a crow. It was my job to watch the offering to make sure it was a crow that took the food and not another type of bird or animal.

I found a place to sit at the top of the stairwell from the house to the roof. It was shaded enough for me to stay cool while still allowing me to watch the plate. Every once in a while, I would have to leave my corner to shoo away other birds. The crows were not coming as quickly as my hungry stomach would have liked. As time passed, I began to think about where I was in life and where I wanted to be. The truth was, I was scared of my default future. I knew that if I took the job at the factory, I could maintain my family's life; but I also knew it would mean that I couldn't make their life better. Engineering college could make our lives better, but I didn't have the financial means to pursue that future.

My family was counting on me. I was finally old enough to fulfill the duties my father had left behind when he passed. They were waiting for me to step up. We had borrowed money for my sister's dowry six months prior.

Since then, we had been living with a debt that my family expected me to pay back now that I was out of junior college. I had also met a wonderful human (Vijju, now my wife) I wanted to spend my life with, but I didn't know how to provide for her, either. On that rooftop, I began to cry. I looked down at my feet; they were dirty from the walk to get the brahmanaas. My clothes were sweat stained from sitting on the rooftop. I was just a dirty man with no light at the end of the tunnel. Above, the crows were circling. I was a victim of my life, waiting for it to happen to me.

Until I decided I wasn't.

As the epiphany began to take hold in my mind, my head lifted and my heart began to race. I felt I was on the brink of a transformation. A chill ran through me. I had one life to live. I could use it, or let it use me.

I decided I was not okay with my default future of running a shop in my small native town or working in a factory. I was not okay with the bare minimum my family had been living with. I knew I had to do something.

"You can do this, Jeet. You are going to figure out how to make life better," I thought with determination.

It was around this same time that a crow decided to fly down and take the offering from the plate. I could no longer sit around and wait. I retrieved the empty plate and went downstairs to join my family and break my fast. I felt confident and excited. I had clarity.

I let my mother know I wouldn't be taking the factory job. "Don't worry about the future, Ma. I am here and I will figure it out," I told her.

Just as something inside me broke the day of the mango juice, on this day in 1992, something opened up for me. Life opened up. I became present to the life that was possible when I took responsibility for my own potential – and embraced my potential for greatness. I shifted from the mentality of "Why me?" to "Why not me?"

All of the things that had happened in my life up until that point shaped me into the man I had become. I was clear about what I needed to do to create many things in life. I became very committed in that moment, the fog lifted, and I became a responsible man. Instead of thinking,

"Why did my dad have to die and leave me in this position?" I thought, "My dad died, and thank God that because of it, I grew into a person who can be resourceful."

Thank God I had to be responsible. Thank God I had to be smart and work hard. If my dad hadn't died, I would most likely still be in Nagar, probably working at one of the many street-side shops. There is nothing wrong with that life. It is a respectable life. But my impact would have been limited.

I was accepted into the engineering college two months later and humbly borrowed money from a friend to pay tuition. By the time school started in January of 1993, I was in control of my life. I was up to something big. I was going to make an impact.

Do you want to make an impact in your world? Are you ready to take responsibility for your life and get to know yourself at a deeper level? Are you ready to create something that will make a difference in the world? And are you ready to celebrate life for all that it is and can be?

Come on this journey with me.

First, we will explore. Exploring is the internal, intellectual work of looking within yourself to identify your strengths, weaknesses, opportunities, and areas in which you are stuck. It includes looking at relationships and your presence in other people's lives to discover how you are and if that differs from how you want to be.

Then, we will accept what you discover. If you can't accept it, then look at what is coming in the way of shifting from "Why me" to "Why *not* me?"

From there, we will commit to create. Creating is taking all the work you have done on yourself and putting it into action. It is showing up as who you are committed to being. It is being intentional with your interactions and your relationships as you interact with the world around you. Creating that life requires courage: the courage to be who you want and the courage to develop new skills.

And finally, it is time to celebrate. Celebration happens after you explore and create. It is seeing your work pay off. It is the proof that you have authentically created an impact. It is the creation that happens because of YOU.

Throughout this book, I will share my own stories, lessons learned, and insights acquired, as well as stories from people I have met.

SELF-REFLECTION

Identify an area of your life where you most wonder, "Why me?"

What is a way that you are learning or growing in that area? How can you flip it to "Why not me?" How can you grow from it?

What is possible in your life once you move from "Why me?" to "Why *not* me?"

EXPLORE
Part 1

Find Internal Peace to Create Your Future

> "Eventually, you will see that the real cause of problems is not life itself. It's the commotion the mind makes about life that really causes the problems." – Michael A. Singer, The Untethered Soul

That day on the rooftop, I finally discovered my motivation to live a life that was both ambitious and fulfilling; yet, I had not found my peace. By that I mean that, while I was committed to taking my new path, my actions were still clouded with doubts, fears, and stress. I did not fully believe in myself or trust my ability to realize my dreams. I was driven, but I didn't know where I was going.

That peace came years later, in 2007. But before I tell you the rest of my story, I want to tell you another story about my friend and co-founder of In Time Tec, Dan Puga.

When Dan was eight years old, his parents divorced. The experience left him feeling confused and unworthy. Looking back, he says that, from that point on, his life became about proving his worth to others. His concern about being worthy of others' esteem, love, and affection manifested in different aspects in his life. He felt he had to be smart, capable, and independent in order to be loved by others. As he grew older, that desire to be worthy turned into a need to "show you how good I am."

As a child, while looking through his father's yearbook, he saw his dad had been valedictorian of his graduating class. He asked his dad what that meant, and his dad responded, "I was the top of my class; I got the best grades in school." He could tell his dad was proud of this accomplishment. That really stuck with Dan: being smart was good. He thought that meant that his parents would be proud of him if he was successful in school, so he worked hard academically. Some subjects came easily (math), while others he struggled with (he often wondered why he had to take a drama class). And though he was working hard, he was not at peace. If he perceived a threat to his intelligence, he acted out. After all, he used his intelligence to earn love from his parents. So anyone smarter than him was threatening his very need for love. This lack of peace lasted his whole life and caused a lot of noise and suffering around him.

Dan met his wife Candi while in kindergarten. They were quite the teenage power couple in their small town, but, as sometimes happens, they got pregnant. Dan could have taken this news as a burden. For him and Candi, life as they formerly knew it — the life of carefree teenagers basking in the glow of their first love — was over. He could have given up on his dreams and aspirations and dropped out of school, but he knew this would have made his life harder in the end, not easier. He didn't want to settle down as a struggling teenage parent (although to be clear, parenthood at any age can be a struggle). And he was committed to being responsible because he had something to prove to the world: that he could make it work for him and his family.

So he and Candi got married and moved to California so he could attend college. Dan needed to show that he could support a family, finish his education, and begin an impressive career. And he eventually did all that. But at the time, he was motivated by the all-consuming need to prove his worth. He was surviving, but he was not thriving.

Dan's need to prove himself did not diminish with success. As he entered his twenties and then his thirties, this burden continued and even grew. His competitiveness grew with it.

"My superiors at work loved me," Dan explained to me. "They knew I was an intelligent guy who would work hard to get things done. The people who worked for me loved me. They knew I was in their corner and would fight for them. But my peers hated me because I was always competing with them or pointing out when they were wrong."

Dan found that proving himself in his personal relationships was even more difficult. He would use sarcasm and intellect to make his peers feel small in order to build himself up. And at home, he held his children to an impossibly high standard because, after all, they were a reflection of him.

Looking back, Dan describes himself as volatile. He remembers that his wife was always walking on eggshells, afraid to set him off about small things.

Sadly, he was like that for most of his life: quick to anger and then quick to apologize. He used his intelligence to dominate everyone around him. He was constantly evaluating and criticizing others because he was constantly evaluating and criticizing himself. His relationship with his daughter, Angela, was especially strained. He remembers a time that he got angry at Angela and her friends and yelled at them while they were hanging out in her room.

When he stormed out, his daughter turned to her friend and said, "He will be back. Just wait." And he was. Dan came back within thirty seconds and apologized for his outburst.

"Wow. How did you know he would do that?" her friend asked.

"He always does." Angela said.

When I met Dan, he was thirty-seven years old and still very much the same person I just described. But I saw something beneath the volatility. I saw a loving, caring human with no inner peace. Without inner peace, he lacked the ability to consistently express the love he had in his heart.

Yet I sensed his potential and the greatness he could achieve with his life when I started In Time Tec with him and Sandeep, Matt, and Rakesh.

Those first few years at In Time Tec were not easy: starting a business never is. But Dan's rigidity made it even more difficult. We butted heads constantly. But I was committed to Dan and his life.

However, it took several years for me to broach the subject with Dan himself. One must tread lightly with volatile personalities. About two years after I met Dan, I found my opportunity. After a meeting, we were taking turns putting on a little putting green in our small shared office in Nampa, Idaho. He was quite angry about the meeting. He was quite angry at the people who had been in the meeting. He kept talking about how he would show them how smart he was. But the next moment, he started excitedly telling me about some fun plans he had made for that week." I sensed that he may be open to talking about things that might otherwise make him feel uncomfortable.

"Danny, do you know you were very up and down with your emotions and reactions in that conversation earlier?" I asked him.

"Yeah, I know," he replied.

"Do you know that being like that has an impact on people?" I asked.

"This is just the way I am. It is in my DNA. My dad was like this too."

"I get it. Your dad was like that too. But do you like it that way?" I knew he didn't, but it was important that he admitted that himself.

He paused for a moment. "No."

"And you are sure there is nothing you can do to change it?"

Another long pause. "No."

This admission was key: he knew he was unpeaceful, wanted to change, and yet didn't see a way to do so.

"Hmmm. Okay," I said. I had planted the seed of change. That was enough for now. I didn't want to push him any further, so I set aside my putter and left the room.

I knew what was in his heart. I also knew he needed to find his own way to peace. So I continued to work on myself. I knew that my credibility and leading my life by example would finally help Dan discover his heart the way I had discovered mine years prior. So I started showing up for him in different ways. I offered resources in the form of books, articles, and courses I had found helpful in my own journey. I redoubled my efforts to ask him thoughtful questions that might resonate with him, that would help him get to know himself and help me get to know and understand him. My questions danced around his volatility. I made sure to never agree or disagree with his approach to life. I always came from a place of love.

One day in 2013, we were both attending a leadership development program in Seattle. Through the program's content and our personal conversations that day, Dan started to see what was possible for his life.

Since then, Dan has been peacefully building a future and creating leaders around him. He is no longer burdened by his fear of looking stupid or incapable, or by a need to prove himself to everyone. Over the last several years, his contribution to our company and to the people around him has expanded exponentially. Some people in our company used to be afraid to talk to him. They avoided him in hallways and meetings. Those same people now go to him when they see a gap in leadership and need guidance. And they don't leave his office crying anymore.

Dan's journey took years of introspection, exploration, and creation. The most important journeys cannot begin and end in one single day. However, through the years, he has found peace about what happened to him in the past. And it all started the day we were putting in our office and he finally acknowledged his lack of peace. So how did he do that?

He was not born without peace. No human is.

Humans Are Born Peaceful

Babies are not born with worries or complaints about life. They might feel hungry or cold, but even those physical discomforts do not quite register as "complaints" in their still-forming brains. According to Canada's most research-intensive hospital, Hospital for Sick Children (SickKids[1]): "Up to about eight months of age, your baby can feel anger but they generally cannot be 'angry at someone' because they do not understand when someone is deliberately thwarting their goal."

Essentially, babies can detect when something is not right (e.g., they are hungry), but they cannot assign blame. That changes at around nine months, when they begin to understand that other individuals can affect their desires and goals.

Though we are born peaceful about the world around us, we begin to understand from a very young age when there is a reason to worry. We have experiences that leave deep marks in our brains and hearts, and ultimately shape our development. Because of these traumatic events, we reach adulthood assuming that our worries and concerns are just a way of life. However, that is not the case.

Many studies have explored the effects of these everyday worries and concerns on our bodies. The effects range from chemical imbalances in the brain, to cardiovascular disease, to suppressed immune system functionality. Our bodies are not meant to carry worries and concerns. Our natural state is peaceful.

I do not mean that it does not take work to get to this peaceful state, or that once you find your peace you will live in a constant state of Zen. Rather, I believe the goal is a way of living that will allow you to continually work through worries and stress as they impact your life, so you can ultimately be free from these everyday burdens.

There are two words in Hindi that are almost identical except for one letter, or dot:

- Chinta (चिंता) = worry

- Chita (चिता) = funeral pyre

I find this similarity striking. The first, "worry," burns you while you are alive. The other, "funeral pyre," burns you when you are dead. "Chita" represents your final death, but with "chinta," you die every moment while living. You are burning your life away and not living in the present moment. When you have worries and concerns, you have no inner peace. Without inner peace, your impact will be limited.

When you find your peace, you are able to do what you desire and enjoy doing so without worry. You can also fulfill obligations you don't enjoy without complaints. Your mind is quieted from the constant chatter of what could have, should have, would have. Instead, you are able to live in the moment as a peaceful human being and view every situation from a perspective of open exploration.

Take a moment to reflect on some of your current worries. Make a list below:

_____

_____

_____

_____

_____

_____

_____

_____

_____

_____

How Loud Is Your Mind?

Although humans are born peaceful, life creates a lot of noise in our heads. There is a quote at the beginning of this chapter from the bestselling author and mindfulness practitioner Michael Singer. His book, The Untethered Soul[2] (which I highly recommend reading), explores the origins of the little voice in your head: the one constantly judging, feeling emotions, creating thoughts, and evaluating the world around you.

This little voice is what is disquieting your mind and robbing you of peace.

Let's do a quick self-evaluation to reveal where you might be lacking peace. Take some time to thoughtfully consider the questions below. Write down everything that comes to mind as you explore them. These thoughts can reveal a lot about the worries that are getting in the way of creating an impact in life.

- Is there tension in any of your relationships? With friends, family, co-workers, etc.

- Do you have areas of your life where you feel you just can't win?

- What conversations are you currently avoiding?

- What feels like a burden?

- What feels unfair?

- What are things that bother you the most?

- What do you tell yourself when you are not happy?

- What keeps you up at night?

- What are you holding on to?

What Are You Holding On To?

Now, it is time to dig a little deeper. Every human carries the memory of experiences that left them feeling burdened, restricted, or hurt.

Maybe someone played a prank on you in middle school that left you suspicious of others' intentions. Perhaps you were homeless for a time, so you are now protective of anything you earn. Or maybe, like me, a parent passed away and left a large hole to fill.

There are countless ways life can play out and there are countless more ways you can interpret and internalize the circumstances surrounding these pivotal moments. For Dan, his parents' divorce caused him to wonder if people loved him. From then on, his whole life was ruled by the need to prove himself to people. This is why he was so dedicated to his academics and why he climbed the corporate ladder at such a young age. He wanted people to love him and he thought the only way to earn that love was to prove he was worthy of it.

My lack of peace came from losing my father at the age of two in a society that centers family life, prestige, and economic wealth around the patriarch of the household. For the first twenty years of my life, I was resentful that my father was not around. I felt less than my friends with fathers. I was waiting for my life to happen until that day on the rooftop, when I transitioned from being a victim to taking control over my life.

But my journey had just begun. For the next fifteen years, until I was thirty-five, I was still shouldering my worries and concerns everywhere I went; the only thing that truly changed was that I was taking responsibility for them. I was no longer resentful that my life was not being taken care of by someone else. I was taking care of my own life now. But it still felt like a burden.

I worked hard to take care of myself and my family with love, yet I still didn't feel free or peaceful. This was because I made decisions out of fear: fear of not having enough money, fear of letting my family down, fear of not being successful. I was still burdened by the absence of my father because I was struggling to be everything I wanted him to be if he were alive. That wasn't a conscious choice I made — it was an idea that took root in my mind over time and created noise in my life.

It wasn't until I attended a personal development seminar in 2007 that I was able to find peace about my father's passing. I remember it was a Saturday in January. I was in the second day of an intense weekend of discovering myself and understanding my past. The seminar was held in a large, gray room with no windows. There were about 120 other people there, all seated in neat rows. We had already spent thirteen hours in this room the day before and were back for another thirteen-hour session.

The session was scheduled to start at 10 a.m. I showed up early and sat in the second row. Shortly after 10 a.m., a few attendees were still coming in and finding their seats. The instructor started talking about integrity and why it is important that the whole group be on time. He was letting them take responsibility for being late. The topic dominated his conversation for an hour. I was frustrated — so frustrated, in fact, that I spoke my mind.

At about 11 a.m., I stood up from my chair and said, "I was not late. Most of the people here were not late. Why are you wasting my time because a few people were late?"

"Who the heck are you?" said the instructor. "I am going to do what I'm going to do, and if you don't like it, then leave."

I couldn't believe it. How could he talk to me like that? It's not my responsibility for other people to show up on time. I grabbed my bag and started packing up to leave. When I got to the door, the people who were late asked me to stay. Shortly after, the instructor told me I was being selfish about only producing results for myself and not taking care of the people around me.

For me, taking responsibility of other people was still a burden. It reminded me of being a little boy with the responsibility of taking care of my mom and four sisters. There was no peace. I was always responsible and produced results, but it was because I felt like I had to. I knew that if I didn't, I would let down the people who were counting on me. It had been a burden ever since my dad died and kept me from feeling at peace.

When I got present to the fact that if my dad had not died, I would not even have had a possibility to be who I am today. I may not have had the ability to take care of the people around me. In that moment, I took a deep breath and let go of every resentment and burden I carried in my heart about my father.

For the second time, I was incredibly thankful to him for being gone — not because I didn't want him in my life, but because I was finally aware of how powerful and resourceful I had become because of his absence. I was someone everyone else could rely on, and I wanted them to. More importantly, I wanted to spread that sense of pride, calm, and competency to others. I saw a future in which my life was much bigger than just me, and I welcomed it. My responsibilities to myself and others were no longer burdens. Those burdens became blessings.

Although it began with my father, that shift in thinking soon cascaded down to every worry and concern in my life. I had finally identified the need that had not been met when I was younger, and by identifying and facing it, I had freed myself of it.

Behind each of your concerns, there is also some driving need that is not being met. In order to change the patterns you are stuck in, you too must take a deep breath, engage in meditative reflection, and be truly honest with yourself about the fears and long unmet needs that drive your behaviors.

Now Is the Time to Free Yourself

Now it is time to circle back to the list of worries and concerns you created. For each one, ask yourself the following questions:

- Why is this concern okay or not okay with me? Why do I have this complaint?

_____

_____

_____

- What do I need that I'm not getting in life right now?

_____

_____

_____

- Why do I need this?

- When did this first become a worry or complaint?

- What do I want from myself or others in order for this complaint to go away?

The final question I want you to answer is this:

- Who have you become because this happened?

On your list, there are likely to be traits that you find useful and other traits you feel bogged down by. All of them are simply two sides of the same coin. Because of my need to become the "man" in my household from a young age, I became extremely disciplined and hard working. This also means I have a hard time slowing down, which can be overwhelming for people when they first meet me.

Because Dan was driven by a need for acceptance, he is incredibly perceptive. That means he is also the first to point out when something is wrong, which can come across as nitpicking.

It is important to own both sides of your coin. Use the traits that move you forward in life to your advantage and use the traits that feel negative sparingly. If you take responsibility for them and use them wisely, they can both come in handy as you are creating your impact. Once you take responsibility for them, they are no longer burdens. Instead, they become tools you can use to fulfill the life that you want.

What does this look like in action? Look closely at what you consider your burdens and find the positive traits. Then reframe the burdens as blessings. Take a look at a few examples below:

Burden	Blessing
My parents got divorced because I was not good enough.	My parents' divorce caused me to work hard and accomplish things in life.
I was abandoned by my father.	Not having a father around made me responsible and disciplined.
I did not make the sports team.	Not making the team allowed me to focus more on my studies and my grades improved.
I did not get good grades in school.	I struggled with tests, so I became very hardworking and secured a great job.
I was fired from a job.	Being fired forced me to become an entrepreneur, which allowed me to make a greater contribution.
I struggled being an entrepreneur.	Struggling as an entrepreneur made me appreciate and love people so I made a bigger contribution in my community.

Think about the difference in those statements for a minute. Let's say you were the child whose friends played a mean prank on you, which has left you with a lifelong suspicion of others' motives. Own that! Being suspicious can mean you are more in tune with the people around you and might make you really good in business meetings. You are able to pay attention to the details, and that allows you to make a difference for yourself and others. By recognizing that your worries and concerns stem from past needs that weren't met, you can fully recognize who you have become as a person — and who you have become is beautiful.

Take a moment to make a list of some of your personal burdens and

Burden	Blessing

then reflect on how they could be a blessings:

It is important to understand that while Dan has become a more peaceful person, he still has triggers. There are still moments in his life when his need to be the most intelligent person in the room overrides all other considerations and desires. However, he values his peace and the person it has helped him become so much that he is able to quickly overcome that trigger and recenter himself.

I, too, have triggers where new projects and challenges can come across as a burden. We all do, because we are human, and taking accountability for the past does not erase it. But now, I listen to my internal voice and ask myself, "What are you worried about, Jeet? You are way more capable than you were in the past. Working on a new project is an opportunity to express yourself. It's truly a blessing and I'm ready to take on the new challenge." Whether we succumb to those triggers or overcome them is a matter of viewing each event as a possibility to grow. Don't resent what happened to you in the past; those traumatic moments don't define you. The past doesn't get to decide your future. Take responsibility for your past and own it. Owning it provides you with choices.

And making new, bold choices is the first step toward finding your peace. It allows you to discover your true needs and values without the messiness of the past getting in the way. When you accept your past as a blessing and become peaceful with it, you are ready to create the future you want in life.

The future cannot be predicted, but futures can be created.

— Dennis Gabor

SELF-REFLECTION

Identify a time you were most peaceful and happy? What made that moment so peaceful for you?

_____
_____
_____
_____
_____

What were you able to create around you in that moment?

_____
_____
_____
_____
_____

If you were like that all the time, what could be possible for you?

_____
_____
_____
_____
_____

Identify Your Needs

"As a person sees into her blind spots, she realizes that the ego hit of accomplishment isn't the same as success itself."
–Dave Logan, John King, and Halee Fischer-Wright, Tribal Leadership

Now that you have acknowledged a lifetime of unmet needs and, through them, found precious peace, how do you keep it? The next step is to understand those needs, which will allow peace to be more present in your life.

Growing up, I didn't have much; I was very familiar with scarcity. If I had a need that was left unfulfilled because of my family's lack of resources, it caused me emotional pain. I learned to avoid that pain by keeping my needs to a minimum. However, there were certain things I needed beyond food and shelter. Like most human beings, especially children, I needed to feel like I belonged. I was the only boy in a house with five women, and being at home often felt like a burden. I did whatever I could to get out.

If you meet me in person (which I hope you do at some point), you might notice that my right ring finger is bent at an odd angle. I injured it in a cricket accident when I was thirteen years old.

That afternoon, sometime in April of 1984, a group of us were practicing on the field in front of my high school. I was in the outfield when the batter hit the ball my way. He hit it pretty high, so I ran and looked up, trying to predict where I could position my hand best to catch the ball and ... I missed. In cricket, outfielders do not wear a glove and the ball is very hard, much like a baseball. So, when I missed, the ball hit my finger directly. It hurt, but it just felt like I had jammed it. I didn't think it was broken, so I kept playing.

Eventually, when the excitement of practice wore off, my finger started to hurt. But our small medical facility did not have an X-ray machine, and there wasn't much to do but splint it, anyway. That injury didn't sway my love for the game. I could have given up that day. But, while cricket is a very popular game in India, for me, playing it was an obsession, a need. I needed an outlet for all my energy. I didn't have brothers I could wrestle with or a father to teach me the more masculine skills. Cricket provided a sense of belonging and a sense of worth. A broken finger was not going to stop me from fulfilling that need.

Growing up, I had my basic needs met, even if they were not met in glamorous ways. We always had food to nourish us and a place to live. I had hand-me-down clothes and used schoolbooks. So instead of needing the best things, I learned to be content with what I could accomplish. I didn't have the best cricket gear, but I became the best player. I didn't have the nicest schoolbooks, but I became one of the smartest people in my classes. Not focusing on getting more or better things to fulfill my needs freed up my focus so I could create more around me.

Long before I broke my finger, I had come to terms with the fact that my family could not afford nice cricket gear for me. And, looking back on my need for cricket gear versus my need to play the game, I see how one need overriding the other shaped me as a human. I probably couldn't articulate it as an adolescent, but I instinctively understood which needs are integral to my self-expression and which needs are actually just wants in disguise. Once I acknowledged this vital differentiation, it became a wonderful tool I continue to use in my daily life.

Maslow's Hierarchy of Needs

I am fascinated with Maslow's Hierarchy of Needs. In 1943, American psychologist Abraham Maslow published his theory about motivation of human behavior in a paper titled, "A Theory of Human Motivation.[3]" Now known simply as Maslow's Hierarchy of Needs, it is presented as a pyramid, starting with basic needs like food, shelter, and sleep at the base. At the peak of the pyramid sits self-actualization.

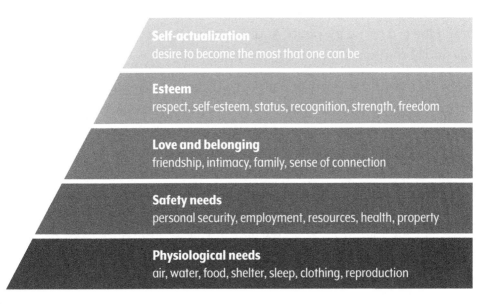

Fig. 1 Maslow's Hierarchy of Needs

As you can see, the first two levels are considered basic needs. Physiological needs are at the bottom and are considered the bare minimum required for a human to stay alive. Safety needs are on the second level and include shelter and physical safety. These two levels don't leave room to focus on anything other than raw survival. These needs are easy to meet for most readers of this book as compared to our ancestors, or even those living in developing parts of the world. For the most part, money is the key to keeping these two levels of needs met. If you have money, these basic needs are all but guaranteed. You are motivated to have money to fulfill these needs because they ensure your survival.

The next two levels of Maslow's hierarchy are considered the psychological needs: love/belonging and esteem. These are the needs that tell you to dress a certain way in order to be accepted, or to work hard in order to be recognized, or to buy fancy things in order to be respected. When you are working toward these needs, you are actively living your life.

These are the needs I will focus on in this chapter because my goal is not just to help you live your life, it is to help you thrive in it. In order to get there, you first must understand your psychological needs. The better understanding you have of these needs, the more likely you are to reach the top of the pyramid. And the top of the pyramid is where you will finally create a long-lasting impact.

In the first thirty-five years of my life, I was driven to try desperately to not only fulfill my basic needs, but also my mid-level psychological needs. When I got good grades in school, my family paid attention to me. When I was good at cricket, I was popular and other kids wanted to play with me. When I became successful in my career, my paycheck reflected that, and my family was proud. However, because I never addressed my unmet needs of being loved and admired, I started to act like a "tough guy" as I proved my worth. This was because I was driven by the fear that accompanies unmet needs; I felt I needed to protect what I had built, while ensuring I wasn't letting down the people who depended on me.

This way of living became more and more limiting to my future and those around me. I stopped giving people the space they needed to thrive because I was consumed with fulfilling my own needs.

Back before I started In Time Tec, I worked at a big corporation. My superiors there would give very similar feedback at every performance review: *You need to let other people take things on, let people lead, listen more.* I didn't understand the feedback. I wanted to do all those things myself because I thought I was the best at doing everything. If I could do everything, why would I stop to let others do a worse job?

My perspective changed one day in 2008 when I was attending a company leadership retreat in Singapore. This retreat focused on teamwork — how to interact and partner with other people. We broke into six teams of eight to ten people and did an activity where we raced to build a wooden frame. The faster we built it, the more capable of producing results we would prove to be.

We each started with individual pieces, but it didn't take long for me to take over for my team. I probably did ninety percent of the work in that exercise. I didn't give the space for anyone else to help because I was so concerned. I wanted my team to win, at any cost. I have always been competitive, but on this day, I had no willingness to lose the game. I took over because I didn't want to depend on my team members. I was not sure if they were capable enough for our team to win. Our team finished first in the exercise. I was thrilled, and I assumed my team was as well.

But after this exercise we had a feedback session about everyone's experiences. One of my team members shared with me, "Jeet, you did not even let me play. I did not get to have any contribution. You didn't even give me a chance and I didn't learn anything from this exercise."

This feedback led to one of the biggest and most transformational moments in my life. I realized how narrow and rigid life would be — and how unhappy and frustrated I would be — if I spent all of my time and energy only concerned about my own needs and not the needs of others. On my flight back home from Singapore, I realized how much I was not letting people learn and grow around me in the interest of my desire to win. I attributed winning to being loved and respected by others, but I realized how stingy I had been.

I only cared about fulfilling my needs, and didn't care about other people's needs around me. I have a lot of capabilities and know that I can produce results, but now I am always looking to include others in that process. I focus on bringing people together. I still have a need to be loved, but I have learned to fulfill that need by loving people, rather than producing results. It used to be about me; now it is about others.

Don't Confuse Feelings or 'Wants' with Needs

Before my epiphany, I was passionate about taking care of my own needs and those of my family. I was a grumpy, angry man because, up until my mid-thirties, that was all I thought I was responsible for. And I refused all help to see to these important tasks.

The middle two levels of Maslow's pyramid are where emotionally charged needs live. If your significant other suddenly stops loving you, you feel abandoned. If you find out that someone was saying negative things behind your back, you feel hurt. On the other hand, if someone compliments you on your nice car, you feel pride. If you pay the bill at dinner with friends, you feel satisfaction at being able to afford the gift. When I was ferociously fulfilling my own needs, I was not taking into consideration how emotionally charged they were.

Both positive and negative emotions drive the desire to fulfill needs on these middle two levels. Those emotions can consume your life, like they did mine. If all humans worried about feeling happy all the time and making sure everyone liked them, the world would not progress. If they all felt protective, the world would not progress. So instead of focusing on not having any psychological needs, focus on *why* you have them and how they fit into the life you are creating.

If I continued to live life as I was — focusing on the wrong needs, not making space for others — I would not be writing this book today. And I remember vividly when I saw my need for recognition as it truly was: a burden.

That pivotal moment happened when I was working for the big corporation I mentioned earlier. A meeting had been called by a peer. It was a big, high-stakes meeting. About ten people were in attendance: lead engineers, a marketing representative, and people from the firmware, hardware, and software teams. We were looking for insights into hardware limitations, an area in which I was a domain expert.

My peer began the conversation and talked for five minutes. For the other fifty-five minutes, I talked. I took over. Through my words, I made everyone else feel small. After that meeting, a peer I cared about deeply and had immense respect for shared with me how I had come across to others: possessive. I thought I was being passionate, but that passion had become a problem. When I thought I was making a difference by generously offering my insights, I was really just trying to meet my own psychological needs.

That check-in from my peer made me stop and evaluate my needs. *Why did I act that way?* I knew working hard was good, and I knew gaining knowledge was good — but to what end? Who was it serving? The answer was singular: myself. I was only taking care of other people when I had to, and that responsibility had become another burden. This was not who I wanted to be. I genuinely wanted to take care of other people. I thought I was, but I was not. Because overriding that desire was a consuming need for love, belonging, and esteem. I didn't even consciously know I needed these things, and yet I was living my life to find them.

And there it was. The shift to awareness. I knew I needed recognition, and knowing that made it my choice. I had identified it and taken its power. As I mentioned earlier in this chapter, once you have control and understanding of your psychological needs, you can finally move to the top of the pyramid: self-actualization. And this is where you can create an impact.

At the beginning of this chapter, I quote a book by Dave Logan, John King and Halee Fisher-Wright. In it, they explore the different levels of leadership, which very much align with Maslow's Hierarchy of Needs. The authors define five different stages of leadership, exemplified by the following mottos: "Life sucks," "My life sucks," "I'm great," "We're great," and "Life is great." They argue that half of all people live in the level-three stage: "I am great."

Forty-nine percent of people are driven by their need to be recognized for their own individual successes and accomplishments, and most of them get stuck there. The authors describe an epiphany that must happen in order to move up to the highest levels of leadership. Just like in Maslow's pyramid, once the first four stages of leadership are understood and those needs are met, leaders "level up" to stage five: "Life is great." This is where you can start to make a big impact. This is the stage where humans move from good to great, and where companies move from competing with others to recognizing the infinite potential and their ability to make an impact on history.

That is where I am going to take you because it is where I have been.

What Is Critical?

Now that you know what the journey to the top looks like, it is time for some self-reflection so you can start taking your own steps to get there. It is time to determine which needs are critical to your life and what is keeping you from creating your impact.

Evaluate Everything

Have you ever spring-cleaned your house? If so, you probably ritualistically cleaned out the often ignored and hard-to-reach spots. Of course, it doesn't have to be done in the spring but it is known as the most complete cleaning session of the year (or decade, depending how often you do this).

That is what I want you to do with your psychological needs: conduct a spring cleaning. Bring all your psychological needs front and center. Then take advice from organizing consultant and author Marie Kondo: "Keep only those things that speak to your heart. Then take the plunge and discard all the rest. By doing this, you can reset your life and embark on a new lifestyle."[4]

If you are unsure where to start, here are some examples:

Relationships

- What do you need from your family?

- What do you need from your friends?

- What do you need others to need from you?

Material possessions

- What do you need from your living quarters?

  _____

  _____

  _____

- What do you need from your vehicle?

  _____

  _____

  _____

- Why and how often do you need to eat out?

  _____

  _____

  _____

Emotional needs

- How often do you need to be alone or be around people to recharge?

  _____

  _____

  _____

- What kind of recognition do you need from your peers? Why?

  _____

  _____

  _____

- What do you need people to say about you when you are not around?

  _____

  _____

  _____

For each one of these needs that you identify, ask yourself the following questions:

- Is this need critical to stay alive?

  _____

  _____

• Is this need serving a purpose in my life?

_____

_____

_____

• Is this need allowing me and others space and freedom to create an impact in this world?

_____

_____

_____

• Why do I need this?

_____

_____

_____

• Do I need to look good or feel good?

_____

_____

_____

• Do I need it to express myself fully or to create something?

_____

_____

_____

• Does this feel like a burden?

_____

_____

_____

This kind of deep reflection might take a while. You have built an entire life around these needs. But while you are evaluating them, you must also understand why you have those needs.

Note: a printable worksheet with more comprehensive list of questions is available at abundantcoach.com/ resources or you can scan the qr code at the bottom of this page.

Understanding Needs Shows You How to Meet Them

Why do you need to understand all of your needs? So you can identify them for yourself, articulate them for others, and ensure they do not become a burden. More importantly, you must be intentional about how you are spending your time and energy if you are someone who really wants to be more, do more, and have more for themselves and those around them.

For example, I have identified that I need to pay a little more money to fly business class instead of coach when I travel internationally. It used to be that I thought people who flew business class had really made it in life, and I wanted that feeling. But when I began to fly business class, I discovered that it allows me to sleep comfortably on a long flight so that when I arrive at my destination, I can go directly to work and start contributing. It might seem like I feel the need to look good, but I have found that it actually allows me to operate at a higher level more quickly, which benefits my business, our employees, and our clients.

The goal here is to become intimately familiar with what each need is adding to your life. Use your needs — do not be used by them. If you need a certain amount of alone time to recharge, understand and articulate how it helps you show up more fully the following day. If you need your spouse to acknowledge you, understand what that does for your relationship. I actively ask my wife, Vijju, to acknowledge me, because it is important to me that she sees what I am doing for our family.

How Much Is Too Much?

Of course, I could always fly first-class. Those tickets cost more money, but the seating provides more legroom, entire beds, and more amenities. However, I don't really need any of that. It is a nice-to-have.

You see, it is important to also understand your threshold between "need" and "nice to have." If you have identified that your house is too small for your family, be conscious of how you go about trying to find a new house. Do you really need the 4,000-square-foot house in the nicest part of town that would put you in an unreasonable amount of debt? Or would the four-bedroom house in the neighborhood across town that is in your budget create the same quality of life for your family?

You must be aware of your needs threshold. It is a slippery slope from "needs" to "nice-to-haves" and many people can get caught up in the downhill slide into "looking good" and "showing off." And remember, people who want to look good and show off are just focusing on the emotional side of their psychological needs.

Someone on my team has three dogs that she loves like they are her human children. It is important to her that they are taken care of. For the past six years, she had been living in a house with a yard. However, her circumstances recently changed and she moved into an apartment. While living there, she was spending more than two hours a day walking her dogs because she no longer had a yard for them to run around in.

She realized this was taking up a significant amount of her time and made changes to her life to be able to afford a place with a yard again. She doesn't need five acres; while that would be nice to have, it is not her need. She found her threshold.

Most needs in the middle two levels of Maslow's hierarchy are an emotional fulfillment rather than a reflection of what you are quantifiably accomplishing in life. Once you are peaceful, you will find that most of your emotional attachment to your needs disappears and it will be easy for you to evaluate and understand this level of needs.

Remember, there is nothing wrong with having needs. They are necessary to live and survive. But in order to thrive, you need to "level up." And you can't do that without fulfilling those needs in the middle.

Fulfill Your Needs

Chances are, you have already developed a way to meet your psychological needs. And through our work, you now have a deeper understanding of them. So what do you do when you hit a point where they are not fulfilled?

I shared earlier about the employee who needed a yard for her dogs. In order to fulfill that need, she moved in with a friend so she could pay off her car and have extra money in her budget to eventually afford a house with a yard. She went from a two-bedroom apartment all to herself to a small bedroom in a house shared with three others. She also cut out all her unnecessary spending and wasn't as social during this time. She shared with me what she was doing and told me she would work hard to earn more money as time went on. She was very dedicated to this fulfillment. It seemed like a sacrifice at the time, but not having a yard weighed more heavily on her.

Let's say your current car isn't reliable and you have decided you need a new one. You have identified the car that would suit your needs while not overdoing it. What are you going to do to get it? You could get a car loan and, as long as that fits into your budget and doesn't become a burden, that is a perfectly reasonable option. You could also save money by cutting down on eating out or shopping. Or you could figure out a way to raise your income by asking for a raise or getting a second job.

The point is, if you understand your needs at a deep level and are trying to fulfill them, ask yourself: have you done everything and more that is in your capacity to fulfill that need? If not, you will have a complaint and will be unpeaceful.

What about instances when you cannot fulfill a need? How do you keep your peace? Accept things as they are for now and find a way to ensure your self-expression matches what you are creating. Using the car as an example, if you cannot afford another car, could you find an affordable mechanic to keep it running? Can you learn to maintain it yourself?

Have you done everything and more to fulfill that need and it is just not possible, and you have accepted it and still don't feel you are able to be self-expressed, what then? Go back to chapter one and find a way to be peaceful about it.

After all, the goal in life is to continue to progress, to climb up Maslow's pyramid. You must first take care of your basic needs and understand your emotional needs before you can live the life you want. How do you do this? You must thrive rather than just survive. Take time to ensure you are prepared to show up fully for others. In order to thrive at the top of Maslow's pyramid, you must be ready to share what you stand for and express your values openly.

SELF-REFLECTION

What was your biggest complaint about your needs growing up?

Where are you operating on Maslow's pyramid?

What actions can you take to get to the next level of the pyramid?

Express Your Values

Up to this point in the book, you have done quite a bit of deeply personal work. It takes courage to look at your past and identify why you are feeling unpeaceful. It took humility to set aside your ego and look at your true needs with clarity. You needed to do this in order to move to the next steps in your journey toward creating an impact.

I acknowledge all the work you have done so far. And yet, you are just getting started.

In this chapter, we will talk about the values you hold as a human. If you were living on this planet alone, you wouldn't need values. You need values because you interact with other human beings, and they need to know what they can count on you for. They need to know who you are so they fully understand the foundation of your relationship and what they can expect of you.

While peace and needs are about you, values are about others — yes, others. While they are your values, conveying them to others is how they fully understand who you are. In order to be an effective communicator, leader, coworker, friend, and loved one, you need to be able to express your core values to others.

According to a report in Nature Human Behaviour[5] from August of 2017, "Personal values are subjective in nature, and reflect what people think and state about themselves. Consequently, both researchers and laymen sometimes question the usefulness of personal values in influencing action. Yet, self-reported values predict a large variety of attitudes, preferences and overt behaviors. Individuals act in ways that allow them to express their important values and attain the goals underlying them. Thus, understanding personal values means understanding human behavior."

Justin, an employee at In Time Tec, grew up in a small farm town on the border of Oregon and Idaho. It was a quiet place to grow up, with more livestock than people, and where family and hard work were paramount. As the youngest of four children, Justin had many people before him setting examples of how to live life through his core values.

When I first met Justin, he had come to our office to have lunch with our Vice President of Business Development, Paul, and talk about potentially joining our team. The two had first met when Justin was a trainer at the gym Paul frequented. They invited me to join them for lunch.

As we showed Justin around the office, he greeted everyone with a warm smile and a firm handshake. We then found a quiet conference room to talk about life, what Justin wanted, what he was committed to, and the kind of person he was. I could tell within minutes that Justin was someone with strong values that were a guiding force in his life. I saw someone who was hard working, disciplined, and committed to contributing to the world around him.

Of course, we hired him. When I recently asked him what his values were, he did not hesitate: "Well, the first thing that comes to mind is the four core values at In Time Tec: trust, transparency, integrity, and leadership. Beyond that, my values are family, hard work, and doing for others what they can't do for themselves," he said.

I could have guessed his values. You see, because of how openly and purposefully Justin lives his life, others have experienced his values; he proves them through his actions. He shows up for every person with the same presence; they know exactly how and when they can count on him. Anyone in our office could ask Justin to help move a couch on a Saturday and he would show up, no questions asked.

He is the kind of person who will (and does) stop in the middle of traffic to help someone whose car has stalled or has a flat tire. The experience that he exudes to both those he knows personally and strangers he encounters is hard work, love, and contribution. That kind of person, one so incredibly rooted in their values, is empowered to create a huge impact in their world and bring others along with them.

What Values Guide You?

You may already have a list forming in your mind of the values that guide your life. You might have values that your parents passed down to you. Or maybe you experienced something traumatic that caused you to run your life by values opposite to your upbringing. Everyone has an idea of what is important in their life. Let's take a closer look at what is important to you.

First, ask yourself the following questions:
- What can people count on you for?

- Who do you admire and why?

- What qualities do you look for in others?

- What do you expect from others?

• What makes you angry?

• What are you proud of?

• What makes you feel safe in conversations, relationships?

• What do you look for in others to engage in a relationship with them? (Leaders, companies, romantic partners, friends.)

• What do people say about you? (Pro tip: Actually ask people what they can and cannot count on you for.)

• What are you a stand for? (Learn more about being a stand for something in Chapter 10.)

Write this list down and find the similarities. Do you gravitate toward people who are honest? Do people describe you as trustworthy? What are some of the themes?

My word of caution is to beware of creating a laundry list of values. Too many values create noise in your own head and can cause confusion and tension with other humans, especially if your multitude of values is in opposition to their own.

Do Not Become Boxed in by Rules

One big distinction to make as you continue this journey is the difference between values, principles, and rules. I pulled the following definitions from the Oxford Dictionary:

- *Value*: a person's principles or standards of behavior; one's judgment of what is important in life.

- *Principle*: a rule or belief governing one's personal behavior.

- *Rule*: one of a set of explicit or understood regulations governing conduct within a particular activity or sphere.

They are related, and yet these three words have vastly different meanings when put into practice. Values are your understanding of what is important to you in life — something that you are ready to give your life up for. Principles are how you think you should conduct yourself in certain situations. Rules guide the actions you take to ensure things work seamlessly.

Let's take a traditional family dinner, for example. Your values instill in you that family is important; a principle is that you will attend a weekly family dinner with those you love; and a rule is that you will bring a dish to share every time. Rules are the structure that show others our values: by bringing a dish to family dinner, you are showing respect and love for those who are attending.

That isn't to say that rules are rigid; dishes can be homemade or store-bought, they can be main dishes or side dishes, they can be appetizers or desserts. Or, if you are running late and don't have time to bring anything, people will understand because rules are flexible. Human life is about standing for something but allowing enough flexibility in your mind and heart that change will bend and not break you. Our future is unknown by design, however, by being clear on what values, principles, and rules guide your life, you will be the most prepared to meet whatever your future holds head on.

Here is another example of how the three intertwine in a real-life situation. My wife does not eat meat. This is a religious belief that she holds dear. One of my values is love, and because one of my values is love, a principle I have — or a behavior I have chosen — is to not hurt people whenever possible. And a rule that I have created out of that principle — or how I conduct myself in certain situations — is to also not eat meat.

In this example, my rule of not eating meat is not a burden and I don't make others wrong when they eat meat. In fact, when we get together with a group of people, we order meat for others to eat. My rule is simply an expression of my love for my wife, which is one of my values. However, rules can become a fixed way of being if you don't understand the principle and value they are serving.

Rules and principles are intertwined and can bend and change with time, situations, and perspective. But your values should remain steady. They are the bedrock on which you live your life and others relate to you.

Take a moment to write down your own values and principles/rules below:

Values	Principles/Rules

The Experience of Values

When you are clear on your values and live your life expressing them, you create a shared understanding with the people you interact with. Imagine you are in a coffee shop on a rainy day. At the table next to you is a blind person with a guide dog sitting at their feet, reading a book in braille. They ask you what the weather is like. You could tell them, "It's wet out there!" which is a common enough expression, however, in this situation, that doesn't convey very much information.

"It is currently pouring outside," you say instead. They nod and tell you they are waiting to leave until the rain lets up. About fifteen minutes later, the rain starts to slow down. You lean over and tell them it is just a light drizzle now. They thank you, put their book away, and head toward the door.

"Pouring" and "drizzling" are both words to describe the rain. However, one paints a picture of heavy raindrops coming down in steady streams, while the other describes small droplets coming down lightly. And for the blind person sitting beside you at the coffee shop, this distinction makes a huge difference. They cannot see what is on the other side of the window and rely on your words to determine what kind of experience they will have when they step outside.

Similarly, values create an experience for those around you.

Some of my own personal values are on the walls of the In Time Tec offices: trust, transparency, integrity, and leadership. When I thought about starting the company in September of 2008, it was common in the business world to talk about company core values. I knew whatever business I started had to have strong values that I could use in my professional life.

I sat down at a small table in my apartment in Bangalore with a notepad and began brainstorming what was important to me. I went through a list very similar to the one earlier in this chapter. I thought back to my childhood and what kind of values served me well. I remembered how earning the trust of my neighbors meant that I always had someone looking out for me. I knew that when I tried to hide anything from my family, it always made whatever I was hiding worse. I recalled what I had learned from courses I had taken as an adult through which I had discovered that, without integrity, nothing works for long. And finally, the common thread through all of that, and through my life, was an underlying commitment to leadership, no matter where I was or what I was doing.

About six months after writing down these values, Matt, one of my friends and a co-founder of In Time Tec, was tasked with creating the website for the company. We met via Skype and talked about what we wanted people to know about In Time Tec. I shared with Matt the values I had written down in my notebook before. I shared what I thought the company's core values should be and how I had landed on those values.

After I shared, Matt was thoughtful. He asked, "Are you sure? Is that what you want to write on the website? They look fancy and I really like them, but I have seen companies write these kinds of values down and then not live up to them. Are we actually going to live this way? Because once we write it down in a public place for all to see, we have to hold ourselves accountable."

With all of the confidence and assurance I had in me, I told him that yes, we were going to live these values. And we have been embodying them ever since.

When new employees join In Time Tec, they join a learning group that meets for an hour once a week. They are a part of that group for a year; the purpose is to share with them the experience of our company values and support them as they learn to become that experience for others.

We know we don't live in a bubble. Employees and clients are critical to doing business. By understanding and embodying our values, we are able to share with others who we are as a company. But more so than that, employees and clients are able to experience who we are.

I recently asked Michelle Haynes, head of talent management and a growing leader in our company, what her values are. "Love, leadership, and creation," she replied, fairly quickly. I asked her why those are her values. She paused for a long moment and said, " I have gone about my life with a sense of these things, and I thought I knew why until you asked."

I sat in silence with her while she really did the intellectual work to figure out why those are her values.

"Those values came from an absence of those things growing up. It wasn't that I wasn't loved, it was that I thought the love was tied to accomplishments. So I want to be unconditional love for others."

I asked if people were experiencing her love. The most important indicator that you are living your values is that others are experiencing them.

"No." She replied. "Not always. When I have a need that is not being met, my values show up differently."

She completely got it. These lessons all tie together. She is now aware that when people are not experiencing her values, she needs to think about what psychological need is not being met.

Over the course of your life, your circumstances, experiences, and priorities will shift. Likewise, your principles and rules are constantly evolving and need to be periodically reassessed and nurtured. Take time to revisit them once in a while to look at how they show up in your life. Your principles and rules should never be a burden. They should always feel like a possibility: the possibility to create something new through that strength and conviction. If something is no longer applicable to your life, get flexible. Throw it out, if needed. Only keep what inspires you and works in your life. It is better to adapt than to be stuck with what is no longer working.

"We make a living by what we get, we make a life by what we give."

— Sir Winston Churchill

SELF-REFLECTION

Ask others how they experience your values. Does this match up with how you view your values?

_____

_____

_____

_____

_____

Identify someone in your life whose values are easily identifiable. What can you learn from this person?

_____

_____

_____

_____

_____

What are things that get in the way of you living by your values?

_____

_____

_____

_____

_____

Learn to Be Flexible

> **"** *The measure of intelligence is the ability to change."*
> *– Albert Einstein*

I can't help but smile as I sit down to write this chapter. When I outlined this book, I was in India, on a work trip that had been significantly altered due to the sudden appearance of the COVID-19 pandemic in March 2020. I had originally planned to stay in India for about a month; I was going to celebrate our company's anniversary at both our Jaipur and Bangalore locations and lead a series of leadership offsites.

However, barely two days into our first offsite, the rapid rise of COVID cases pushed India into lockdown. I, along with dozens of our company's leaders, had to scramble to get back to our homes or find a place to stay during the lockdown. Since we didn't know how long it would last, I took shelter at my friend and co-founder Sandeep's house in India. All domestic and international flights were canceled. My family was still back in Idaho. So we waited. There was no way of knowing how long the lockdown would last or the impacts COVID would have on the world. I certainly didn't have a say in the matter – none of us did.

I was a guest at Sandeep's house in India for two months. It was not what I had planned, nor what I had wanted, but it happened. And I, along with the 500-plus people in our company, found ways to be flexible during the global crisis.

There is not one person in this world who was not affected by the virus in some way or who didn't have to adapt to the new norm, so I know you can relate to my situation. We all had to adapt, to become flexible. We learned to use Zoom if we didn't know it already. We had happy hours over Zoom. We held virtual baby showers and attended virtual classes. We shifted meetings to accommodate kids who were now home during the day and became very forgiving of the crying babies and barking dogs in the backgrounds of calls.

Even with the stress, despair, and sickness that permeated the world around us during the pandemic, even as we lived through waves of quarantines and lockdowns, we found ways to appreciate the small joys in life. We touched base with family more often. We went for walks. We took deep breaths and embraced an uncertain future.

I smile as I write these words now, knowing how the timing worked out with the creation of this book. Flexibility became the world's daily default and yet, life still happened. The global pandemic was a perfect example of the importance of flexibility in life and in creation.

During my quarantine in India, I saw many posts on social media about people discovering new hobbies, or about others who finally got the time to recharge and reset their lives. Despite all the hardships endured and lives upended, humanity still found ways to remain positive and create beautiful impacts during a time of global crisis.

This shows how important it is to be flexible in your life. You can be peaceful and be very clear about your needs and values and the world will not care. No matter how hard you try to be intentional with your purpose and create an impact in this world, the stars don't always align in your favor. And during those times, your ability to be flexible will be the driving factor that keeps you moving toward your goals.

How to Get "UnFixed"

The opposite of "flexible" is "fixed," as in a fixed way of being. Look at the physical world around you and you can see plenty of examples of this. Look at a healthy tree and you will find the trunk is firmly fixed in the ground. It is immobile, inflexible, held firm by a root system that can run both deep and wide. But the limbs and the leaves of this same healthy tree are very flexible. You'll notice that when the wind blows, the trunk stays sturdy while the smaller limbs sway and move.

Then there is the wonder of glass, a substance that is moldable while hot and keeps its shape once cool. Even your muscles are flexible when used and stretched often, or can be tight and immobile when not used or stretched properly. However, if you keep using your muscles, your body will adapt to new movements and abilities.

In all of these examples, there is a possibility for a flexible way of being and a fixed way of being. When the object is fixed, there is no opportunity to create something new; conversely, if the object is flexible, there are many ways to grow and become something more.

With the example of the tree, the leaves and seeds being flexible create the opportunity for more trees. If the seeds were fixed to the tree, or if the branches and leaves did not bend with the wind, there would be no way for seeds to disperse on the breeze and create more trees.

With glass, when it is hot and moldable, you can create whatever you would like; but once it is set, the only way to create something new is to shatter it or heat it to make it flexible again.

And with your own body, if your muscles are flexible and in use, you can explore new sports or hobbies. If your muscles are stiff from lack of use, it is harder to try new things and your potential to explore a new activity is hindered.

Being fixed is not inherently bad, but I hope you can see how a fixed state limits creation.

In your life, there are certainly areas where it will serve you best to be somewhat fixed — your values, your commitments, and honoring your word, for example — and there are areas in which it will serve you to be flexible to different situations, circumstances, and input. If you are really committed to creating an impact in your world, you must remain flexible. Otherwise, your fixed way of being will hamper your intentions and progress.

I once mentored a woman who told me she needed at least ten hours of sleep in order to be productive. She was in her thirties and seemed healthy enough, and even though she was very strict about her bedtime, she still had very little energy during the day. She was very fixed in this mode of being and would not consider exploring another bedtime or curtailing her sleeping hours.

One night, this mentee and I attended an awards ceremony with a few other people. The ceremony was over at around 8 p.m. and the group decided to grab a late dinner at a spot across the street from the awards venue. It was a gorgeous summer night in Boise. The skies were a dusty pink and the temperature was ideal for patio drinks and snacks.

At around 9 p.m., my mentee mentioned that she was feeling tired and it was approaching her bedtime. The conversation among the group had just started to take off and some amazing creation was happening, but my mentee was too fixated on her bedtime to notice or care.

A few minutes later, she announced to the group that she had ordered an Uber and it would pick her up in mere minutes. I was shocked; we were all a bit dismayed. It seemed that the only thing that mattered in this world was her inflexible need: her very strict bedtime. She didn't consider the impact her leaving had on the group. She didn't consider all of the conversation avenues and ideas that were left unsaid and unexplored because she was not willing to be flexible.

I want to take a moment here and say that her need for sleep is not bad. Maslow recognized it as a basic need. Of course everyone needs sleep to survive. She truly did need to sleep that night, as did we all. And we all eventually made it to bed. However, she didn't pause to examine why that rigid need overpowered everything else that evening.

Her need for sleep on such an uncompromising schedule was in direct opposition to what she had committed to that night: an evening with her colleagues to celebrate, bond, and create. I knew that she was committed to being a loving and peaceful leader. I knew she was up to big things and actively working on creating her impact. Yet her inflexibility dampened the group camaraderie that evening and diminished my opinion of her as someone I could count on. How could I trust her to be a leader if an emergency arose, when I knew she would call it quits promptly at 9 p.m.?

She left that evening, got her ten hours of sleep, and didn't think anything of it. A few months later, we reflected on that night and began to explore why she had that need for such a strict bedtime. Her immediate response was to be expected: "Because I am tired."

"Got it. Are you truly tired though, or are you being lazy?" Perhaps this could have been phrased more tactfully, however, I tend to be very upfront and blunt with the people I have been mentoring for a long period of time.

Fortunately, she was not insulted by my bluntness. "Um ... tired," she said, after pausing to truly consider the question. "I have a lot going on in my life and it takes a lot out of me."

"Okay, I see. That evening after the ceremony, you left before everyone else even though the conversations were becoming very meaningful. Do you know the impact that had on the group?"

She replied that she hadn't even considered the impact of her leaving. I explained that leaving so abruptly that night had shifted how the rest of the group saw her. They now viewed her as someone who was rather selfish and not committed to the creation of team unity. They also saw her as someone who was uninterested in contributing to compelling conversations. These opinions from her colleagues would hurt her ability to become the leader and creator that she aspired to be.

She then explained to me that her bedtime routine allows her an opportunity to reset, reflect on the day, and generate her mindset for the next day. She knows that if she doesn't get enough sleep, it affects how she functions and what she is able to contribute. I truly appreciated hearing her perspective as it helped me understand this value she held that was so foreign to me.

I then helped her see that we were engaged in an "and" conversation. Meaning that by being open to flexibility in her sleep schedule, she could have created something very meaningful with the group that night and that sharing her need with the group could have made all the difference in how they viewed her.

In the end she understood that she could and should have adjusted her schedule to contribute to the creation conversations that night, or made sure everyone was aware she needed to leave early beforehand. After our conversation, her fixed attitude about sleep no longer outweighed her commitment to contribute and create with her colleagues. She introduced flexibility into her life in a way that allowed her to fill her need while also remaining true to her commitment to be a loving, peaceful leader.

How to Recognize What Is Out of Your Control

Stephen R. Covey wrote about the "circles of concern and influence" in his book, *The Seven Habits of Highly Effective People*.[6] The "circle of concern" includes everything you might be concerned about, for example, finances, social injustice, family, the government, world peace, and tasks at work.

The "circle of influences" is nestled inside the circle of concern and includes what is in your control: your finances, your family, and your tasks at work, if we borrow from the list above. In his book, Covey shows how proactive people very deliberately operate within their circle of influence. As they grow their effectiveness, the circle of things they have influence over grows larger.

By focusing your energy on influencing what you have control over, you can make a much bigger impact than by expending that same energy worrying about the things you cannot control.

Similarly, by being flexible about what you cannot control, you find new ways to create an impact and emerge as the powerful human you are. For example, if you have a fixed understanding about how people should raise their children, you will always be upset when your children have friends over. How the children behave will be inconsistent with how you think they should be raised. But if you are flexible and understand that there are many ways to raise children, you will not waste your time and energy on things you have no say in.

In the story about my mentee, she had control over her sleeping schedule and could alter it as needed based on what she was up to creating. However, she was living her life as if her bedtime was fixed. Once she became more flexible about her schedule, she was able to show up powerfully, no matter the time of day. Being flexible helped her understand what she could and could not control. She now approaches more situations with a flexible mindset.

As you look at your own life, make a list of things you can control and a list of things you cannot control. My list looks something like this:

Can control	Cannot control
• My finances	• The weather
• My eating habits	• Other people
• My fitness	• The government
• My family's safety when they are in my home	• Taxes
• My relationships with my co-founders and employees	• Global pandemics
• My wardrobe	• Death
• My actions	

The list of things I cannot control is not long, but it is extensive. It can seem a little overwhelming. For a moment, imagine the time and energy you could spend worrying about the things on that list. It would be exhausting. It is even more exhausting to think about being fixed about any of the things on that list. How ridiculous would it be if you tried to be fixed about death? If, when your time came, you simply said, "No thank you. I am not ready." Life (and death) doesn't work that way.

Below, take a moment to make a list of your own personal circle of influence. The things you can control and the things you can't.

Can control	Cannot control
• _____	• _____
• _____	• _____
• _____	• _____
• _____	• _____
• _____	• _____
• _____	• _____
• _____	• _____
• _____	• _____

Turning Lemons into Lemonade

When I used to play cricket growing up, we would travel by bus from town to town to play in tournaments. I didn't have money for a bus ticket at times, and yet there was no way I was going to let that stop me from playing. During these times, I would climb on top of the bus, or hold on to the back for thirty-or-so-minute rides. I was so committed and loved the game so much that I became incredibly flexible in my approach to travel and did whatever it took to get to matches.

The things on my list that I could not control were very broad, general things that the majority of humans have no control over. There are also smaller things that we encounter every day that we cannot control: hitting all the red lights on our commute to work; long lines at the grocery store; the attitude of the customer service representative at the bank; the bird that left a present on your newly washed car.

However, we do have control over how we react in these situations and the language we use to express ourselves. We also have the ability to examine situations and see what else is possible, what else can be achieved. I believe some people call this "turning lemons into lemonade."

Getting frustrated or angry that things are not going your way is a surefire way to stifle yourself and prevent any possibility of creation.

In fact, it is probably a great way to cause destruction. When you are stopped at a red light, you could get frustrated. And you may carry that feeling to your first meeting of the day, and the other people in the meeting will feel that tension coming from you. How do you think that will affect your meeting? I can tell you from personal experience, entering a meeting in a bad mood does not leave much chance for a positive outcome. Your colleagues may not relate to you as someone who can be counted on to act professional when the situation calls for it.

Consider what happens if you could keep your cool at that stop light; perhaps you take a calming breath and call the people with whom you are meeting to let them know you will be a few minutes late, and to reiterate your excitement about the meeting. They will both feel respected and reassured by your professionalism, instead of being distracted and put on edge by your negative emotions once you arrive.

Let's take a look at the difference between flexible and fixed reactions in other situations:

Situation	Fixed	Flexible
	Reaction	
	Anger, make a rude comment to the cashier about needing more registers open.	Understanding, empathy toward the cashier about how hard they are working.
The line at the grocery store is long	*Outcome*	
	Ruin cashier's already hectic day. Carry your own anger home.	*Make the cashier feel appreciated, no negative feelings to carry home.*

Situation	Fixed	Flexible
Rude customer service representative	*Reaction*	
	Be rude back	Show compassion but ask to speak to someone else.
	Outcome	
	Your day is ruined.	*Protect your positivity and get your problem resolved.*
Branch blown onto car	*Reaction*	
	Get angry and take it out on the insurance representative.	Understand that there are things out of your control and it is no one's fault.
	Outcome	
	Carry your anger and frustration with you until your car is repaired.	*Live with peace while your car is being repaired.*
Concert being canceled due to weather	*Reaction*	
	Pout about it, rant about it on social media.	Find other ways to spend your time and support the artist.
	Outcome	
	Force everyone around you to be subjected to your frustration.	*Get a new t-shirt and a refund on your ticket.*

Situation	Fixed	Flexible
	Reaction	
Sudden death of a loved one	Let your sadness overwhelm you and impact your day-to-day life.	Acknowledge the life that was lived and the contribution that person made to you.
	Outcome	
	Fall behind in life while you are in mourning.	Celebrate life.

Notice how being fixed in each of those situations is a dead end to negativity, which is no place to create an impact. Instead, by being flexible, you create alternatives that leave others feeling positive and yourself feeling peaceful.

The more you negatively react to situations that are out of your control, the more you wear down your own power.

By working through frustrating situations, you retain your power instead of relinquishing it to a situation you cannot control. Alternatively, when you give a situation power, you begin to feel powerless.

• Identify a time your inflexibility got in the way. What could you have done differently?

_____

_____

_____

_____

_____

_____

_____

No Sacrifice Necessary

Let me be clear on one important point: flexibility does not equal sacrifice. In fact, the opposite is true. When you are fixed in your ways, you are implying that nothing is more important than your way. And in doing so, you are forcing yourself (and others) to sacrifice the beauty of limitless possibilities in every interaction and situation.

When I was in engineering college, I used to live in a hostel. That specific hostel held around 300 kids. As you can imagine, a lot of them just wanted to have fun. Because of the circumstances of my life, I was committed to studying. I knew my future depended on how well I did in school. Most of the other kids just wanted to graduate. For me, just graduating was not good enough; I needed to do well.

I was quite focused on my studies, but I also wanted to build friendships. Back in those days we used to hang out until 10 or 11 p.m. We would talk, play cards, or go for a walk. This took away from my studying time and I was torn. How do I take care of my studies while still maintaining these friendships and feeling like I belong? I decided I would finish having fun with them around 10:30 or 11 p.m., and then I would go to bed and get up at 4 a.m. to study. I learned to be flexible. I found a way to be someone who can express my love and have a sense of belonging, and still take care of my needs by finding another time to study. I also found time to take a nap for an hour after my classes and before I met up with my friends. This way my sleep, studies, and friendships were not compromised. That's the beauty of flexibility.

In any relationship, it is important to be open and flexible in order for the relationship to be successful. If one party takes the approach of "my way or the highway," the characteristics that make relationships precious — like love, trust, and esteem — will wither and the relationship will fail. Why? Because life is not a one-way street. If you are chained to your fixed ideas of how life should be, and demand others be chained to your ideas as well, you will soon find yourself alone and constricted.

I have a friend who was living alone when the COVID lockdown hit Boise. When Idaho's governor first announced the lockdown, she burst into tears, afraid of (and already reacting to) a situation that was not even fully realized yet. She deeply dreaded the prospect of living in total isolation, of staying home and not seeing her friends, family, and colleagues in person. Her self-expression was to connect with others and celebrate their lives with them.

She felt she would be sacrificing her mental health and her self-expression if she stayed home alone for weeks – or even months – at a time. Yet, she had no control over the situation.

She reached out to someone who offered her empathy while also helping her see that the pandemic could open up new possibilities for her if only she were flexible enough to acknowledge and explore them. This person asked her, "What can you create during this time that you wouldn't otherwise have time to?"

Just thinking about the possible ways to answer that question helped her relax a little and regain some positivity during a stressful situation.

In the end, during the lockdown, she explored new avenues for love. She and the person she was dating were able to have very deep and meaningful phone conversations because they were not distracted by the normal routine of their relationship, like going out for dinner or meeting up with friends for drinks.

Her triumph in this situation fills me with such pride for my friend. Instead of remaining fixed and wallowing in sadness, she got flexible and discovered a new level of human connection in one of her relationships. Because of her flexibility and willingness to look for another way to create, she also found another way to be fulfilled.

More often than not, flexibility will not require sacrifice and will lead to endless opportunities for creation. However, there are certain experiences where practicing flexibility could run against your values. For example, I am not flexible about eating meat because it goes against the value I shared in chapter three: my love for my wife. If being flexible goes against any of your values, it is a no-go. Remember, your rules and principles are flexible, but your values are foundational and mostly fixed (which is why it is so important to be clear about them

Many people who "go with the flow" will find being flexible easy. Others will have to work hard to relinquish their fixed way of being. Chances are, the people who already go with the flow are also more peaceful than the people who demand things go their way. It is also true that people who find peace more easily are often more flexible as a default. See? It all ties together.

You cannot have creation without flexibility, as creation usually requires others' involvement.

As you continue on your journey, exploration is vital to moving toward creation. The final step in your exploration is to pay attention to every other step by reflecting often.

SELF-REFLECTION

On a scale of 1 to 5, how flexible are you? Do you like where you are? Do you feel free, or constrained? What steps can you take to move in a different direction?

_____

_____

_____

_____

_____

Identify a time you were rigid and missed an opportunity.

_____

_____

_____

_____

_____

Identify a time when your flexibility created something that was not otherwise possible.

_____

_____

_____

_____

_____

Reflect Often

6

> "Life can only be understood backwards; but it must be lived forwards." – Søren Kierkegaard

Self-reflection is one of humanity's greatest, most humbling, and most powerful traits. Our ability to consider our words and actions and how they affect us and those around us is remarkable. It is what makes us human.

Of course, everyone reflects to some extent. Perhaps you analyze your behavior after a party, embarrassed at a joke that fell flat; or recall with pride a work presentation that went well. Reflection is powerful because it is your chance to quiet your ego and consider how you come across to others. When done properly, self-reflection is both humbling and incredibly empowering. I cannot emphasize this enough: It is the key to becoming the very best version of yourself, which is the key to creating a lasting impact in the world.

As a child, reflection was a sort of survival mechanism for me. I mostly used it when life was hard or chaotic and I needed results. Growing up without a father to help guide me through the hardships of becoming a man meant I had to take this on myself. My best tools were self-reflection and cricket.

As I shared in chapter two, for me, cricket was more than just a game. It was a way of proving my worth, to myself and to my community. I was bullied often as a child, and so I was left wondering, "Am I doing something to provoke these bullies? What can I change in my interactions with them?" It's true that with bullies, there's often not much the victim can do to change their behavior. However, I found that it gave me a sense of control and power to consider these questions. For me, personally, the answer was more about focusing on the few friends I had and the things that gave me joy.

When I discovered a love of playing cricket, after each game I had to consider, "What are my weaknesses? What didn't work?" If I didn't improve as a player, I would not get a chance to play in the future.

This self-reflection meant more than simply playing the next game. As a boy without a father, my skills at cricket, and my ability to apply myself and improve my game, helped shape my reputation in my little village. My self-reflection grew. It became, "How can I improve my life through playing this sport?"

I analyzed every game. *Why did I miss that hit? What do I need to practice to ensure I land it next time?* Reflection instilled in me the dedication to work and self-improvement that one day would enable me to provide for my family.

In order to reflect in a truly meaningful way, you must practice it every day, with deliberation. True reflection, and the action that comes from it, not only benefits you — it enhances the lives of everyone you are in contact with.

My favorite time to reflect is when I'm driving home from work. There is something calming and meditative about driving down the road with other commuters like myself. Surrounded by people, yet completely alone, I find myself rehashing my day. I ask myself questions like:

- Did I achieve what I wanted today?

- Did I create what I wanted to create?

- Did I love people?

- Did I show up as confident or arrogant in the client meeting?

- Did I show up as a leader the way I wanted to show up?

- Did I contribute?

Some days, these are tough questions to answer honestly. In the beginning of my reflection process, I found myself making excuses: *Maybe I wasn't as attentive as I should have been in that meeting this morning, however, I didn't sleep well last night and I'm tired. Perhaps I should have played with my daughter when she asked, however, my colleagues were waiting on these emails.*

It's kind of ludicrous when you think about it, the idea of making excuses to yourself or cutting corners. However, when you start reflecting day after day, and when you catch yourself making excuses for your own behavior day after day, a pattern emerges. These excuses are just that: excuses. I am not being honest with myself. In honesty, I am disappointed in my own behavior and I need to do better.

What does doing better look like? First, it means confronting how you interacted with others in your work and personal life and owning up to the times where you fell short.

How was that lunch meeting? Did I take time to understand what my colleague was saying or was I just pushing my own agenda?

How did that phone call go with a friend? Did I pay attention to what they were going through or was I trying to multitask?

How did that client meeting go? Did I show up as a trusted partner or did I push things based on what my company needed and focus on closing the deal?

I no longer make excuses for my behavior. If I fell short of being a good friend or a good colleague, I admit it to myself and take corrective action right away. Sometimes that involves putting my phone on speaker and calling that person during my drive home to clean up an incident that may not have gone the way I planned. Other times, I send a heartfelt email when I get home, or make a mental note to talk to that person differently tomorrow.

There were other times, especially earlier on in my life, when I simply didn't know how to take corrective action. I lacked the knowledge, skills, or tools to help myself be better. Then it became a matter of researching what training I could take, what books I should read, or classes I should enroll in to become a better manager, a better listener, and a better leader: in short, the best version of myself.

Now, these self-reflections end with a sort of mantra, or vow to myself: I need to do better. I know I can do better. And I will strive to do better tomorrow.

Self Reflection, or Mindfulness, Is the Bedrock Practice of Highly Successful People

Obviously, I am not the first to discover the power of self-reflection. Generations of people throughout the span of human history have used the lessons gleaned through self-reflection to improve their lives and their societies. Many highly successful contemporary people openly discuss how it has improved their lives and work.

Microsoft founder Bill Gates practices both mindfulness and meditation daily. He calls his practice "exercise for the mind." On his blog[7], he explained that the practices helped him pay attention and actually listen to the thoughts inside his head. It's easy to believe that for a man that important and powerful, those everyday thoughts, the beautiful and beautifully ordinary core of a person, could get muted by the more consuming tasks of overseeing a successful multibillion-dollar company.

Some of the greatest athletes in the world, including golfer Tiger Woods, basketball players LeBron James and the late Kobe Bryant, and celebrated U.S. soccer champion Carli Lloyd have all openly talked about how reflection, meditation, and mindfulness improve their lives and performance. Not only does it help these accomplished professionals handle the stress and anxiety that can come with performing publicly, but the daily ritual helps anchor them and set them up to compete at their best level. The same athletes watch the videos of their previous games religiously to get better at their game.

It's no coincidence that many people highly regarded in their chosen fields make reflection a dedicated part of their day. While most of us will never co-found a billion-dollar company or become a professional athlete, reflection is a tool available to all, and immeasurably helpful for those who embrace it.

Why Reflection Is Important

Have you ever done or said something that you immediately wished you could take back? Did it make you think with horror, "Why did I just do that?" This happens often to people who aren't in tune with themselves and their compulsions, motivations, needs, and desires. As the Irish poet and playwright Oscar Wilde once wrote, "The final mystery is oneself."

Life is often lived in one of two places: in our heads, or in the outside world. For people who live in their heads too much, the final mystery is how to interact with those living in the outside world. For people who live in the outside world and never reflect, their inner motivations are a mystery. Even if they are successful, how can they be sure where that success comes from? If their lives begin to fall apart, how will they know how to fix it?

By setting aside time each day to explore the great mystery of You through self-reflection, the mystery disappears. You become more comfortable with yourself: with your flaws, your needs, your strengths, and your goals.

Not only are you improving yourself, you are aligning with other human beings. You are understanding what works and what does not work — both for you, personally, and within your role in society at large.

I have a friend who is in the habit of running a few miles in their neighborhood about four times a week. They started running years ago out of vanity, because they noticed their metabolism slowing down. Their pants were a little tighter and they realized they couldn't keep up with their kids anymore. One day, they took some time to consider all that running contributes to their life. They told me, "At my last doctor's appointment, my nurse marveled at my low blood pressure. Getting out and running has helped keep me from feeling sad in the winter." They shared that they have more energy to keep up with their young grandkids than they did their own kids when they were young.

And by running through their community regularly for years, they have gotten to know all their neighbors. When one neighbor lost her dog a few years ago, they ran around hanging up flyers to help her find it. When they sprained an ankle last summer, another neighbor sent his kid over to mow their lawn for a month so they wouldn't have to.

All of this because of running, an activity they took up out of vanity and have been doing without thought ever since. Sure, they knew running was "working" for them, in that it's a healthy activity that was keeping them in shape. However, until they stopped to reflect, they had never taken the time to explore all the ways it had impacted their life or how they, in turn, had impacted their neighbors by being a consistently friendly face. Even if they wanted to stop running, they wouldn't have. It was less about running and more about making a contribution.

Reflection isn't just for the big moments: the make-or-break business meetings, the night before your wedding day, or the birth of your first child. You must acknowledge and analyze every aspect of your life, especially the mundane ones. Because at a fundamental level, even if you are successful — in other words, if you are healthy, comfortable and happy — if you don't understand the roots of that success, you won't be able to continue doing what works. And that is the goal of reflection.

Well, I should say, that is one goal. The greater goal is to not only understand what works, but to be able to increase your functionality, or rather, your human power.

In physics, power is defined as: **Power = Work/Time**

So if you can do good work and do it in less time, you as a person and the system in which you operate will become more powerful. This human power is the rate at which you can convert your dreams to reality. It's the rate at which you convert your intentions into reality. The faster this is, the more powerful you become as an employee, as a partner, as a friend, or as a leader. When a human being is powerful in a positive way, they create that much more.

Remember that this power is grounded in the ability to truly know and express yourself, which stems from reflection. Remember also that you're here on this planet for a finite number of years. Your "T" is limited. In order to get a lot done on earth, you need to optimize your power.

You do this by asking yourself each day, "Why am I here?" And as soon as you understand the answer to that question, you need to begin taking the steps to make it happen. As we've discussed, some of these steps will actually be missteps. And that's okay. Whenever you take action, you're taking a risk that, despite your best intentions and plans, it won't work. And when it doesn't work, what do you do?

You reflect. You learn. You adapt. And then you do it again.

All too often when people make mistakes or fall short, their urge is to brush it under the rug and forget about it as soon as possible, perhaps because of embarrassment. "It's in the past," they like to say. "I'm looking to the future."

How can any of us hope to have a successful future if we do not first confront and acknowledge the mistakes of our past? You reflect, learn, adapt, and then do it again to create a new future.

You may begin the day with good intentions, as we all do. What matters is, at the end of the day, you need to critically examine whether or not you lived up to those intentions. Did you show up as a caring parent, as a loving spouse, as a leader, as a friend?

If you don't reflect, you're not only minimizing your needs, you're diminishing your power. You are becoming inflexible. The questions you have to ask yourself will become harder and harder to answer: "How will I grow? How will I get better? How will I enhance and expand my impact?"

As I mentioned at the beginning of this chapter, self-reflection is the most powerful catalyst for positive change. When practiced honestly and diligently, it allows you to show up each day with love, and to help others navigate their own perceived flaws and missteps in a nonjudgmental way.

Without reflection, there is no growth.

How to Reflect

You may be thinking, "Sure Jeet, you reflect in the quiet confines of your car each day, however, my commute includes a toddler and a pre-teen, which not exactly calming influences. How am I supposed to find the time and space for this?"

The good news is, you can reflect anywhere, and reflection can last as long or take up as little time as you have. You can reflect over your first cup of coffee in the morning, or during those quiet moments when you're trying to fall asleep at night. You can reflect in the shower, or while you're waiting for a bus. You can even reflect amid the noise of a child's basketball game or during a recital. Think of all the moments during the day that you turn to stare at your phone; you can reflect then, too.

The key is intention. Once you have that intention, and have tuned out the noise of outside distractions, ask yourself these questions:

- Are you at peace? Why or why not? What do you need to do to find peace?

- What are you avoiding? What do you feel like you just "survived"?

- What did not work today? Why?

- Were you flexible today? Why or why not? What could you do differently in the future?

- Did you live in alignment with your values today?

- What are your priorities for tomorrow? How are you going to achieve them?

- What did you need today?

- What did others need from you? Did you deliver? Why or why not?

- Did you love/contribute/lead enough?

- Did you spend enough time understanding other people's worlds and perspectives?

• What actions will you take tomorrow? What tools and skills and lessons do you still need to achieve your goals?

Note: a printable worksheet is available at abundantcoach.com/resources or you can scan the qr code at the bottom of the page.

These are the questions I ask myself each and every day — sometimes multiple times a day. They help anchor me when work is intense; they help ground me when my family needs me most. They have helped me to become a committed contributor, a better leader, and a powerful human being. They have allowed me to explore and create. Most importantly, they have reminded me to embrace my mistakes and learn from them so I can show up tomorrow as an even better team player in this game called life.

"Do the best you can until you know better; Then... do better."

— Maya Angelou

SELF-REFLECTION

What actions can you take to make time to reflect every day?

_____

_____

_____

_____

_____

_____

What areas of your life are most difficult to reflect upon?

_____

_____

_____

_____

_____

_____

What can you create by reflecting on those areas?

_____

_____

_____

_____

_____

_____

CREATE
Part 2

Focus on
Others

"

7

"To lose yourself in the service of others may be to truly find yourself." – Mahatma Gandhi

After better understanding yourself through exploration, you are naturally eager to turn your focus outward. Now is the time to begin creating. However, we cannot speak of creation without first understanding the foundation of it; creation requires acceptance of yourself, others, circumstances, and life as is.

If you were living in this world alone, you could completely skip this chapter. However, to paraphrase the English poet John Donne, no person is an island. We come into this world surrounded by humanity and most of us will live our lives this same way, shoulder to shoulder with both loved ones and strangers. In fact, I bet that you want to create in order to have an impact on those around you, from your most immediate circle of loved ones to your community at large. In order to do that, you need to focus on them.

I learned from an early age to focus on others; it was another survival tool for me. Scarcity was so prevalent in my life that I knew my survival was dependent on those around me. I began doing things for my friends, family, and neighbors, and in turn, they looked out for me.

This taught me an important lesson: Your life is not solely yours — it is an extension of the people around you.

A specific memory comes to mind. I was a teenager hanging out at a friend's house when a monsoon hit (which is pretty typical for India in the summer). The streets were instantly flooded and my friend's father was stuck at work across town. He couldn't get home because his motorized scooter was useless in the rain and flooding. However, I had my bicycle with me and I knew it could handle such conditions, so I offered to ride over, pick up my friend's father, and bring him home.

Monsoons in India are not like the normal rainstorms you see in the United States. If you have never been in a monsoon, you have never experienced the relentless beating of rain coming from the sky, or the steadily rising water that floods streets, parking garages, and sometimes homes. It is awe-inspiring and all-consuming. Traffic grinds to a halt and most work stops. It seems that all of life pauses to take shelter during these swift storms.

On this day, there was a lot of traffic backed up for the same reason my friend's father couldn't get home; it was simply too difficult for the vehicles to navigate both the crazy Indian traffic and the crazy weather. I slowly weaved between cars and motorbikes and pedestrians while water was pelting my body and my legs were submerged up to my shins. When I reached my friend's father, the fleeting physical discomfort was worth it. He was so grateful to be able to get back to his family that evening.

He hopped on the back of my bike and off we went, through the same mess of vehicles and rain I had just come through. The trip took a total of three hours but, from that moment on, my friend and his family knew they could count on me. I was someone who would sacrifice my time and physical comfort if they needed me. And in turn, I knew they would be there for me if I needed them.

How Focusing on Others Benefits You

Early in my life, I consumed what others gave me. That is how I survived. I knew, plain and simple, that if I did things for others, they would be more likely to do things for me. I was wholly focused on what would improve my life. I was giving love simply to get love in return. Somewhere, there was a shift in my point of view. I wish I could tell you I knew exactly when it was; maybe it was that day I helped my friend's father through the rainstorm. But that shift pushed me from a consumer of love to a contributor of love.

As I grew older, I learned to focus on others purely for their sake, not what I could get out of them. I began to thrive when I was contributing to the lives of others more so than when I was simply a self-involved consumer. I began to not only feel the warm glow that follows altruistic behavior, but I also began to see my true purpose in life: to wholly contribute to others and not think of myself — in other words, to disappear myself.

Achieving that feeling — the feeling of happiness — has become so elusive in modern society that research about it has exploded. There is now a Happiness Institute, as well as a Journal of Happiness Studies dedicated to researching how lasting happiness is attained. There are college courses devoted to this subject, new branches of psychology are being developed to help people learn to incorporate more happiness into their lives. And yet the answers to the question, "What makes people happy?" seem to be relatively simple: be kind, love others, and help others when you can.

Numerous studies have shown that when you meaningfully embrace altruistic behavior, you feel more happiness[8] in your own life. This same research also showed that self-serving behaviors did not make people happier. The reason is this: helping others gives your life meaning. It gives you purpose. And a feel-good side effect of this is that you, in turn, feel happier.

Remember, life cannot happen without others. Imagine living alone on an island. How would you characterize such a life? Are you thinking to yourself, "I don't need other people?"

My guess is no. My guess is that, given the chance, most of us would act like Chris Pratt's character in the film Passengers: after accidentally awakening from hibernation while traveling to another planet on a spaceship, he awakens another space traveler from her hibernation because he cannot bear to be alone. Of course, that is an act born of desperation: a desperation that stems from being stripped of companionship and community. Because, without those things, who are we? How can we create or give back if we have no one to create for or give back to?

Getting Out of Your Own Way

You should know that, when you realize that serving others enhances your own feelings of self-worth, that is just the first step. Life happens around others. You cannot express yourself to a table, or a tree, or a building. You can only express yourself to other humans. Therefore, in order to live a fully expressed life, you must focus on others. And to do so, you must recognize the selfishness in this world.

Understand that there are two types of selfishness. One is materialistic selfishness. This is all about money, power, and status. Usually, people who are being selfish in this way have an unmet psychological need of some sort (think back to the middle two levels of Maslow's Hierarchy of Needs). This is the type of selfishness that you want to avoid. It's about you, not about others.

Core selfishness, on the other hand, is related to your being. In fact, it is your being. This is all about peace, joy, and happiness. Being selfish in this way is important because it ensures that you can show up for others and be whole and complete. If you don't protect your peace, joy, and happiness, you cannot focus on others.

You'll see both types of selfishness on your journey toward creating an impact — within yourself and others. When you feel materialistic selfishness, try to figure out what need you are trying to fulfill and how to get through it. When it shows up in others, recognize that they are struggling, just surviving in this life. Everyone you interact with is going through their own personal journeys of acceptance and exploration. Their journeys, like yours, are affected by a lifetime of decisions and memories.

Next, remember that there are two parts to every human: your mind and your "being." Your mind is your memories, accumulated over the years, that create thoughts, emotions, and feelings. You tend to act on these automatically, but when you do, you are acting based on past feelings, not who you are in the present. This is where materialistic selfishness thrives. When you act based on your mind, you can get in your own way.

However, you are not your mind. You experience your mind. You are your being. You are your being from the very start of your life. This is permanent. Your being is the source of your peace, connection, and your impact in this world. When you act based on your being, you create possibilities for other human beings. This is where your core selfishness lives. As I said, when you are not peaceful, joyful, and happy, you cannot focus on others. Usually, if you are not feeling these things, it is because your mind is louder than your being. Something is bothering you and, until you fix this, you will not be effective at focusing on others.

Recently, I helped one of my employees separate her mind from her being. A group of leaders were at an offsite in a beautiful mountain town about two hours away from our headquarters in Meridian, Idaho. We were planning for the future of the company, looking inward at ourselves and our own growth, and connecting as a leadership team. Late on the first day we were there, a member of our group had a breakdown. She expressed that there were certain things that were not working for her. She was unhappy, unpeaceful, and had an unmet need. She said she wanted to leave the company. I knew this was her mind showing up in a negative way. She had always seemed to me to be a powerful leader, and I thought she was in it for the long haul. That night, I couldn't sleep. I kept thinking about what I could do to help her get out of her own way. I kept thinking about all the contributions that would be missing if she left the company. The next morning, the two of us had a conversation about what was not working for her and she told me she didn't actually want to leave the company, she wanted to try things differently. We had a wonderful conversation about what that could look like and together, we were able to quiet her mind and let her being shine through.

Now, how do you balance all this? This selfishness and mind and being? You must disappear yourself without losing yourself. It sounds more complicated than it actually is.

What It Means to Disappear Yourself

By "disappearing" yourself, I mean that after you understand the selfishness in this world and have quieted your mind and embraced your being, you release your ego, your daily stresses, your fears, your nagging thoughts of "How is this helping me?" and any other psychological baggage you are currently carrying. Then you should be able to fully embrace acts of altruism and focus on others.

Disappearing yourself is a lot like reflecting. It takes practice. Here are a few check-ins you can use to ensure your mind and unnecessary selfishness aren't sneaking back in:

- Are you listening more or talking more? Asking questions or making statements?

- Are you thinking more about yourself and what you can get out of a situation, or of others' needs?

- Do you spend a lot of time and energy trying to be "right"? Why?

Disappearing yourself is part of the process of creating, which you do for others: your family, your job, your community. These relationships should always be about the other people involved. Examine these relationships closely; how do you view them? Are they filled with confidence and trust? Do they make you feel happy or proud? In general, are they working to the extent that you want them to work?

Remember, it's important not to disappear your being. Your being is who you are. Instead, disappear your mind. Until you do this, it will not be possible for you to focus on others because your mind will want you to take care of yourself.

But Don't Lose Yourself

One pitfall of focusing on others is sacrificing too much of yourself in the process. In the example earlier, when my employee's mind was louder than her being, she felt like she was sacrificing part of herself — her being and her peace — and that wasn't working for her. Just as you must consider the person or the community you're trying to help before you take action, you must extend that same kindness and thoughtfulness to yourself. It does no one any good if your service to others puts you in a place of personal discomfort or pain or causes you to be unpeaceful. Truly good acts come from giving of your whole self and loving another's whole self, not from sacrificing parts of yourself.

You may be wondering, what does it look like to take action and be others-focused without sacrificing yourself?

Being aware of your own boundaries and needs, as we identified in chapter two, will help you know what you're capable of giving as you focus on others. And being able to communicate that is vital.

Let's say your friend just lost her mother to cancer. You want to be there for her and text her an offer to help "in any way you can." You're thrilled when you get an immediate text back, because your offer was made in earnest, however, your heart drops when you read it. She has asked that you take care of her dogs for a week while she makes funeral arrangements and packs up her mother's house.

The problem is, you're afraid of dogs. The idea of taking care of two big, relatively unknown dogs on your own for a week makes you break out into a sweat. You don't know the first thing about caring for dogs and you're afraid of getting bitten. And yet, you've offered your help to your friend without reserve, so now your options are disappointing her in a time of mourning or putting great stress on yourself.

By simply quantifying the help you're comfortable giving in your first message to your friend — "I'm happy to be a shoulder to cry on, or to cook you meals, or help pack boxes if you need me" — you could have avoided this situation.

I talked to many friends and colleagues about focusing on others over the course of writing this book. Many gave me great examples of how they transitioned away from sacrificing themselves in relationships.

• **At work:** "I'm a die-hard team player and I have a problem saying 'no' to coworkers when asked for help, even when I really can't do it. So now when I'm put on the spot, my go-to response is: 'can I get back to you by the end of today?' That takes the pressure off and gives me time to look at my schedule and consider my preferences before I give an answer."

• **In relationships:** "My partner considers doing chores together to be quality time – like, re-grouting the tub. It makes him so happy, and we are spending time together, but it kind of makes me feel like his unpaid intern. It took me a really long time to tell him that I didn't want to spend all my free time fixing up our house. And that I consider more traditional things like going out to a nice dinner to feel more like quality time. Now we do a mix of both!"

• **With friends:** "I had a friend who used to only contact me with bad news or to complain about her life. We'd only go out for drinks when she was single and lonely, or when her parents were going through a divorce. I never heard from her when she was happy or dating someone. I liked being someone she could turn to when life is tough but it also made me feel like a sponge for her negative energy. I eventually told her that I also wanted to be there when things were going well in her life, and that we should be celebrating those times, too."

All of these are good examples of individuals who found a balance between focusing on others without sacrificing themselves. This has allowed them to truly serve others with authenticity.

Focusing on Others to Help

Now that you have an understanding of what is required to focus on others, you can start the process of actually helping and supporting them. And there are two situations that may indicate you can help or support someone: when someone asks for it, and when someone doesn't know they need help. When someone asks for help and you are willing and capable, it's a no-brainer: You should coach them.

A few months ago, I received a message from someone on Facebook. She was a graduate of the same personal development program as me and reached out to me for coaching. I had never met this woman before, but she mentioned that she had heard my name a few times and was interested in the insights I had to offer. Before agreeing to coach her, I talked with her on the phone to make sure I was capable of coaching her in the areas she was looking to improve in. After our first initial conversation, I knew that I could help her, and she appeared to be willing to listen and do the work. I agreed to coach her, and she now comes to my office for one-on-one coaching sessions regularly. After six months of coaching, she has brought her business back on track, lost weight, created a more loving relationship with her daughter, and found a more empowering relationship with herself.

However, when someone asks for help and you aren't willing or capable, you should be honest and defer or refer them to someone else. I once had an employee come to me for help with their mental health. They were having thoughts of suicide and came to me for guidance. I wanted to help, but I knew I was no expert in this domain. I told them if they sought a counselor, In Time Tec would help them share the cost.

It gets tricky when someone doesn't ask for help, but you can see that they need it. In these situations, you should ask yourself questions like:

- Can I help?

- Will this person listen to me?

- Do I have time to help?

- Will they be open for help?

I recently went out to lunch with one of my mentees. She had just returned back to Boise from a trip home to visit her family. As I started asking her questions about how her trip was, I could tell something was missing. It was clear to me that she wasn't complete with her family. She didn't ask me for help, but I knew I could help her. I started asking her questions. "Are you happy with your relationship with your family? What is missing that could make a difference for you? Are you willing to let me help you?" She said yes, and I have been on the journey of coaching her ever since that day at lunch when I saw a gap by simply listening to her sharing.

I created the table below to decide when and if you should help others. If someone asks for help and you are not willing or able, defer or refer them to someone who is willing and able. If they ask and you are willing and able, start coaching them. If they don't ask for help and you aren't willing and able to help them, no action is necessary. However, if they don't ask but you see a gap that you are willing and able to help them with, engage them in a conversation about it by asking questions.

Fig. 2 Jeet Kumar "Asking for Help" table

Sometimes these conversations can get uncomfortable and we will dig deeper into that in chapter eight. But if you are truly focused on others and not yourself, you can make a life-altering impact. Life can expand. A few years ago, an employee from our India office was visiting our headquarters in Meridian, Idaho. I noticed that she was unhappy with her weight and it was often getting in her way. I also knew that pointing out that another person is overweight can be uncomfortable for everyone involved. But what was the clearest to me is that I knew I wanted to help her. I knew how much her life could expand if she were able to find happiness and peace in this area. One day we happened to be in a conference room together. It was the perfect opportunity to start this conversation. "I have noticed that you are not at a healthy weight, are you unhappy about this?" She answered yes, and I helped her start working with another employee who I knew had experience with fitness as her coach and mentor in this area.

I recently checked in with the employee about her experience that day. She shared that she was initially uncomfortable, yet she was willing to change because she knew deep in her heart how important it was for her and the difference it would make. She said that the more time that passed the bigger the difference she saw, and she quickly became glad she did it.

I encourage you to use the table to identify areas in your life where you can focus on others and help. Once you do this, life will expand, and you will begin to see the impact you're creating.

I am still friends with the family I helped during the monsoon at the beginning of the chapter. My friend now has a son in college. He recently reached out to me to see if his son could intern at our company. It made me think about riding through the rain with his father on the back of my bicycle. Back then, I was helping because I wanted to be loved and taken care of. I was a teenager who was just surviving and doing anything I could to be loved. This time, when he reached out about the internship, I was helping because I was living purely in my being and doing anything I could to show up as love for others. The actions were exactly the same, thirty-two years later, but the context was different. In one situation I was focused on me and what I could get out of it, and in the other situation I was purely focused on others.

The moment we begin to truly focus on others, the act of love shows up. It is through our acts of love toward others that we not only create, but we measure our greatness.

The only real prison is fear, and the only real freedom is freedom from fear.

— Aung San Suu Kyi

SELF-REFLECTION

Identify a time in your life when you felt alone. What was that experience like?

_____

_____

_____

_____

_____

Identify a time you made a contribution in someone else's life. How did that feel?

_____

_____

_____

_____

_____

Identify a time when someone made a difference in your life. How did that feel?

_____

_____

_____

_____

_____

Identify someone you would like to make a difference for. What actions can you take to make that difference?

_____

_____

_____

_____

_____

Be Love

> "Love is patient, love is kind. It does not envy, it does not boast, it is not proud. It does not dishonor others, it is not self-seeking, it is not easily angered, it keeps no record of wrongs. Love does not delight in evil but rejoices with the truth. It always protects, always trusts, always hopes, always perseveres. Love never fails." – 1 Corinthians 13:4-8 (NIV)

The previous chapter was about the importance of learning how to truly focus on others and what could get in the way of doing so. That is the foundation of our next step: living with love. You might think you already know what it means to live with love, and likely you do, to some extent. It might mean giving someone a hug when they have had a bad day or telling someone how much they mean to you. But digging deeper, do you really know how to live with love, day in and day out, without fail? Do you really know how to be love as a being?

Love has so many different definitions, meanings, and applications. The ancient Greeks identified seven different types of love: eros (passion), philia (friendship), storge (family), agape (altruism), ludus (play), pragma (duty), and philautia (self). There is physical love and emotional love. There is the love you feel when you are surrounded by friends and the love you feel when you are out in nature alone. There is healthy love and toxic love. There are love languages and love stories.

A few of my friends and colleagues were kind enough to share what love means to them:

> 66 Love means not just showing up, but showing up with enthusiasm for things I know the person doesn't want to do – like having dinner with my parents (they are a bit much). 99

> 66 To me, it means volunteering to do the unglamorous work that most people won't do, like helping administer services to homeless encampments, or clean them up so we don't have disease outbreaks within our homeless populations. These people really appreciate others taking the time to let them know you care. 99

> 66 I would say love means doing something that only you can do – like if you're good at cooking, making a meal for a sick friend, or if you're an empath, volunteering on a crisis hotline. It means knowing what your strengths are and using them to make the world a slightly better place. 99

Love has had many forms in my life. As a child, when I was picked on by bullies, I was concerned with receiving love. I wondered how to get others to see my worth, and how I could create something or express myself in a way that would earn love. Over time, I learned that, if I put others before myself, I would get love in return.

I have romantic love with my wife, Vijju. She expresses her love by cooking, taking care of our two kids, supporting me, and being a stand for my life. I express my love for Vijju in ways that are different, yet more meaningful, to her. Just recently, Vijju wanted to go back and visit her friends and family in India. I happily rearranged my busy work schedule to make sure she could leave the country without any hesitations about our children or the meals we were going to eat. I knew how important this trip was to her and nothing was going to stop me from making it possible.

I have familial love for my children and my immediate family members. This is arguably the very first type of love humans experience, and it is often the strongest. Family will love you in a way nobody else can. I know my mother loved me until her last breath and I will carry that love with me through my life.

My definition of love also includes a commitment to understanding every human. It means getting in the other person's world to know why they are the way they are. I work with hundreds of people, and sometimes that means I am the brunt of someone's negative emotions. Instead of feeling immediately resentful or angry if someone takes their negativity out on me, I try to understand where they're coming from.

One common trait of all the types of love is that they have to be about others — especially if you want your love to create anything. You must be willing to put others' wants and needs before your own. You have to be able to fully identify what other human beings want and how to give it to them.

Love in Action

Close your eyes and picture someone you love. It could be a family member, a friend, or a partner. How do you express your love to this person? How do you make that experience of love for the other person possible? Most of us fall back on words to make this connection with loved ones. It's such an old habit to say, "I love you," that we hardly ever stop to think of what it means. What we're really saying is, "I accept you the way you are."

What motivates you to love other people? Is it out of obligation? Is it about passion? Do you love because you want to be loved in return? Do you love because that's who you are? All of these motivations are valid. Once again, I asked a few of my friends and colleagues — my loved ones — to share their thoughts on why they love:

> ❝ I can't think of a reason why, exactly. Love is just elemental. I just do it, like breathing. Or aging, I suppose. It's just an unstoppable force within me that grows as I know the person. ❞

> ❝ I think there are different types of love. There are definitely people in my life that I love out of obligation. If I'd met them as an adult, I might not have loved them, but they're in my blood, if that makes sense. I can't help it anymore. But as I grow older, love is about looking at someone and seeing the whole person and just wanting to celebrate who they are with them, because they're so awe inspiring. ❞

> **"** Love is about surrounding yourself with people who you can't live a fulfilling life without – who inspire you and support you and help you grow, and doing the same for them. **"**

> **"** When I met my partner it was love at first sight. I can't even explain it. **"**

I cannot find fault with any of those motivations for love. However, I would also point out that most of these are the relatively easy paths of love (and indeed, loving some people is easy). How do you love someone who has violated your trust? Or who doesn't accept some aspect of you, like your sexuality or religion? Love that stems from obligation is a slightly harder path. And yet, I would argue it is intrinsic to fulfilling your potential.

Love begins with acceptance, and until you practice acceptance — of yourself, your situation, other people, and circumstances — you cannot create. Until you can learn to accept and love others, your hands are too full holding up all of the metaphorical garbage, including excuses and your ego, to create. You are hindering yourself.

New Ways to Be Love

We have acknowledged all the typical ways you can be love. Now let's look at some of the other ways you can learn to love. These types of love are creation-based: They are how I create around others.

Show love by caring for people who forward the conversation and are others-focused. These people don't need your coaching or leadership, so just keep showing up for them. Familial love falls into this category, but love as care can be extended beyond just family members.

A man I have worked alongside for the past decade, Paul Perrault, immediately comes to mind as I think about love as care. Paul continuously puts others first and produces results. He doesn't need my coaching. He doesn't need anything from me, and yet I will continue to show up and love him every day. He shows up for others by taking care of them without them even asking. Whether it's hanging a shelf, being the first to arrive in the office and the last to leave, brewing coffee for everyone in the morning, or coming in on the weekends, he looks around, sees the needs, and addresses those needs.

You can also show love by coaching. This is required when someone is others-focused, but they don't forward the conversation. These people are committed and want to make a difference, but they still have inherent needs getting in their way. To show love by coaching, help them develop the tools and skills they lack to begin forwarding the conversation. It may be that they haven't identified their needs and don't know their values. It may be that they are still living a "Why me?" life. Whatever is getting in their way, showing love by coaching is critical to helping them grow.

I am currently working closely with a manager in our company that is completely gotten by our mission of creating abundance. She is so out there in other people's lives, but is missing some tools and skills that prevent her from forwarding the conversation. Because of this, I created a structure where I meet with her daily to discuss how she is showing up as a leader. I watch recordings of the learning groups she has led and provide her with feed-forward. Eventually, the frequency of these meetings will decrease to weekly or monthly, but for now I am doing what's required for her to show love to all people.

When someone wants to forward the conversation but they are not others-focused, you need to show love as leadership. Sometimes the people who need this type of love forward the conversation and sometimes they don't. It depends who they are working with. In this situation, you should coach them. Help them see they can only show up as a leader when they care more about what others want to create and achieve than their own dreams and aspirations. They need to disappear their "I" because it will continue to get in their way.

I am currently working with one of our employees — whom I see so many possibilities for — on how her materialistic needs get in the way of focusing on others. Instead of just telling her to stop caring about materialistic items, we worked on identifying the origins of those materialistic needs. I shared with her how it impacts not only the people around her, but herself and her journey to becoming a leader.

Even tough love is love in action. Keep in mind that you can't offer tough love if you don't first know how to love. Tough love must always come from a place of love. It's for people who are not forwarding the conversation. It's for people who want to run their own agenda and are self-centered. Take a stand for these people.

A few years ago, I told one of my employees that, for the next six months, he was not to bring new ideas to the table. I knew this was going to be hard for him; he constantly shared ideas but did not allow others to share theirs. It was getting in his way. He did it to look good, but it didn't land well with the people he worked with. This employee now is part of our Build In Time Tec Future leadership team. He is a much more thoughtful person now than before we had that conversation.

If you are trying to offer tough love to someone who is not open, walking away is always an option. But before doing so, assess if there is any way to show love as care. If there isn't, have the wisdom to walk away. If you don't, your love will be a nuisance, noise, and a waste. Think of the other person as a wall, and you are hitting your head against that wall. It just leaves you hurt in the end. You should use that time and energy and those resources in other, more impactful, ways. When we exercise the wisdom to walk away, it is truly walking away as love rather than walking away out of resentment.

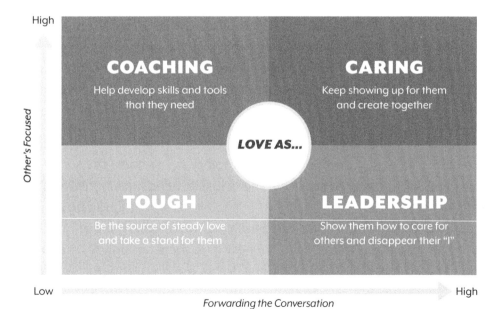

Fig. 3 Jeet Kumar "Love As..." table

Love, when practiced wholly and with empathy, harms no one. It is the purest way to contribute to society. However, it is worth noting that love can indeed be a burden. If one is practicing love selfishly — that is, with one's own needs in mind instead of another's — or practicing love without celebrating the wholeness of the other person, then it is not love. That act is nothing but a shallow, selfish burden.

You can only create if a true form of love is present, and you can only love if others are present.

Therefore, you must consider:

- How do I express myself and relate to others?

- What do/can others expect out of my love?

In order to create, you need a circle of people surrounding you. It's important to be on the same page with these people and have open lines of communication and the foundations to build trust. There must be honesty and respect.

It's true, not every interaction with every individual in your life will be pivotal, magical, or memorable. The stranger you interact with at the airport probably won't look deeply in your eyes and feel your love. Neither will the bus driver collecting your fare. Nevertheless, your interactions with strangers should mirror those you have on a daily basis with your true beloveds: your spouse, your parents, your closest friends.

The hardest moments will be the moments we all dread: firing an employee, ending a relationship, telling a hard truth to a friend. But if you remember the tenants of love in action — that you must try your hardest to understand the human being sitting across from you and work with empathy and love to accept why they are the way they are and why they do what they do — you will be putting love out into the world in the midst of tough circumstances that could devolve into far worse interactions. And isn't that what we all aspire to do? Make the world a little bit better, especially when things are bad?

A World Without Love Leaves No Room for Creation

As we've discussed, it's nearly impossible in our increasingly crowded world to live life truly alone, nor would you want to. But many people find themselves living in isolation or relative seclusion, due to choice or circumstances outside of their control — for example, a housebound person.

What we instinctively know, and what science has confirmed, is that a life lived alone is not a life. The Centers for Disease Control and Prevention even warn that loneliness and social isolation pose a "serious health risk."[9] Research shows that social isolation significantly increases the risk of premature death, rivaling other risk factors like smoking, obesity, and physical inactivity. Furthermore, these isolated individuals face a fifty percent higher risk of developing dementia.

A life lived alone is a punishment. Extensive studies show that when solitude is forced on individuals — such as the solitary confinement used in our prison systems[10] — it causes serious psychological effects including stress, depression, paranoia, hallucinations, psychosis, and even self-harm. Researchers report that isolation is, in fact, just as harmful and distressing as physical torture. While these extreme situations are rare in society, some people simply just choose to be isolated for reasons that can include fear of rejection or letting someone down, or the loss of love.

It is no coincidence that "love and belonging" sits in the center of Maslow's Hierarchy of Needs. Without experiencing love and belonging, none of us would ever reach self-actualization. This is important to remember for yourself, for the decisions you choose to make in your personal life. It is also a good reminder to check in with others, as loneliness is a serious disease with a simple cure. Show up for them as an expression of love. Accept them for who they are and also for who they are not.

Every day presents several opportunities to show up as love. Recently, someone left our company and it left one of our team members feeling burdened with additional responsibilities. I talked with this employee and said, "I know how much you want to do well, and you are taking on so many things at the moment. You need to give yourself enough space and grace to make mistakes. It will all be okay." Showing up as love in this situation left that person feeling relieved and seen.

Another employee recently made a mistake regarding our company's finances. She was very worked up over this mistake. Instead of getting upset about it, I told her, "The past is in the past. You know what you need to do to make it right. Just know you will make more mistakes and that's okay. We will still love you and will always believe you will get it right. You just can't be so hard on yourself." The way that I showed up as love for her in this situation has empowered her and ensured she felt supported.

This year I got news that one of our employee's friend's son had died. The employee wanted to be there for his friend during this time, but he lived in a different state. I shared with him, "Go there. You don't even need to inform anyone. Go do what is required for the people you love, because that is the right thing to do." It is important to me that work doesn't get in the way of our employees being able to take care of the people they love. The way I showed up for him as love in this conversation has allowed him to be peaceful and show up for his friend.

My intention with these stories is not to impress you, but to impress upon you the impact showing up as love can have on other people. Instead of doubling down and micromanaging these employees, I showed up as love. And since then, their productivity and commitment to our company has increased.

Through offsite meetings, one-on-one coaching, and examples like the ones above, I am always asking myself, "What more can I do to be love for others?"

Once we've underscored the importance of love in action, our next goal is finding the best communication tools to convey it. The power of language can help us engage with others on deeper levels and relate to them in ways they understand and appreciate.

"Love does not dominate; it cultivates.

—Johann Wolfgang von Goethe

SELF-REFLECTION

Who needs your love and what could get in the way? How do they need you to show up?

_____

_____

_____

_____

_____

When you love someone, how do you show your love?

_____

_____

_____

_____

_____

How do you receive people's love?

_____

_____

_____

_____

_____

The Power of Language and Action

❝

"Your Words Create the World Around You" – Anonymous

When I moved to the United States, I was twenty-seven years old and had $120 in my pocket. I had never traveled on an airplane before, and the only person I knew in the U.S. was the person picking me up from the airport. If he had not shown up at the airport that day, I would've had no idea what to do with myself. I think back to how naive I was to leave my wife and go to a foreign land where I only knew one person. But I had given my word. I had made a declaration that life could be better for me and others, and I followed my word about moving to the U.S. because I was so gotten by what could be possible for me and my family. If I had decided not to follow my word, odds are I would still be working in my small village in India. Can you imagine how different life would be for me? The entire creation of my company was possible because I said I was going to do something and did it. Until you use language to create your future, nothing is possible.

Imagine trying to negotiate or come to an agreement with someone who speaks a different language than you. While nonverbal communication may offer you some assistance in understanding the other person, there is a good chance neither of you will know what the other person is trying to say.

In the same way, not being able to express your wants and needs and have them be correctly interpreted by others creates several barriers for communication. Growing up with Hindi as my native language, I know the constraints this can cause at times while communicating in English. People want to be heard, and that becomes possible through language. Language is the gateway for communication, and we create and perceive our reality through language.

Think of a newborn baby. When the baby is crying there are several things that could be wrong. The baby could be too hot, too cold, hungry, tired, or uncomfortable. Imagine how much simpler it would be if the baby could use language to communicate exactly what they wanted. This example shows us truly how difficult life would be if none of us learned how to communicate with each other through language.

Now think of your best friend. How did you two become best friends? By connecting through language. When you first met, you were strangers. You got to know each other by talking to each other. Without language, how would you know if you had any shared interests? How would you know if the other person values the same things in a friendship? The simple answer is that you wouldn't. It is through language that the possibility of two strangers becoming best friends is created. Language is the basis of human connection.

How Language Shapes Reality

There are many people in the world who assume that the world is just as we see it: for instance, that an apple will taste just as sweet and crisp, and a sunset appear just as dazzling no matter what you call them.

However, there are others who have long stated that the language we use helps shape our reality. For instance, if you use adjectives like "lazy" and "stupid" to describe impoverished people, and "hard working" and "deserving" to describe billionaires, those words will change your perception of each group of people.

A study conducted by Yale researchers[11] illustrates another way language can literally influence what we see. Researchers used a technique on volunteers called flash suppression, in which a flash directed at one eye functionally limits sight in the other. While the flash suppression was being applied to the volunteers' left eyes, they were unable to see an image that was projected in their right eyes' field of vision. However, when the volunteers were given a verbal cue about the image — saying the word "kangaroo" if it was an image of a kangaroo — many of the volunteers were suddenly able to see it.

This experiment seems to demonstrate that our perception of reality is not as black and white as we might like to believe.

I want you to think of Martin Luther King's "I Have a Dream" speech. Think of how many times you have heard the most famous line referenced in your lifetime: "I have a dream... ." He gave that speech in 1963 and it continues to inspire the masses all these years later. Now think about Mahatma Ghandi and what he did with the power of his language alone. He wasn't violent, he wasn't aggressive, and yet he helped the entire country of India reach independence and end British rule through his words. Creation, no matter how big or how small, becomes possible through language.

I believe the words we and others use to create the world around us help shape our reality, whether we realize it or not. Therefore, it is imperative that we choose our words wisely and with careful consideration of the impact they will have.

At our company we tell our clients, partners, and employees to achieve their dreams through our dreams. I tell every employee that I love them, and I do. We are committed to using language to express our gratitude to our employees because we know that it creates a sense of connection for them. Internally, we don't even refer to In Time Tec as a company. We refer to it as a family because we love our co-workers as we would love our own siblings.

If language creates the reality around us, what can you create through your language? The way you speak your possibilities and goals and intentions into reality will determine how others perceive you. Before you create your impact, how will you tell others about it?

How Language Shifts Your Own Thoughts

Let's say, for example, that you are not very happy or don't feel good about something that occurred. It could be because you let your emotions get the best of you: You yelled at the driver you were passing for driving too slow, or you said some choice words to your husband who shrunk your clothes in the dryer. Reflecting on your reaction results in your being state shifting to disappointment and frustration. You wish you could take it back, but you can't. In these situations, although you can't take back the past, you can create a new future through language.

I remember a time that language shifted my personal being state. I was attending a meeting with one of our partners and I found myself annoyed and frustrated. I was unhappy because they weren't listening and I didn't like the way they were treating us. My actions began to reflect my feelings and I wasn't showing up as who I knew I could be in that moment. My replies in that meeting were getting shorter and shorter.

When I was driving home on that day, I was sad. I was even more disappointed in myself for not taking the high road. I was beating myself up about the language I used to express the words in my head. In that moment, I shifted my being state by moving on from the past. I thought to myself, "When I reach home, I will write an email to our partner from that meeting." So, I did. In that email I explained that I was aware of how I had shown up and it was less than what I believed it needed to be. I then declared a better future by sharing that I will be more open next time they want to meet up. In this example my being state shifted from annoyed and disappointed to empowered and enabled without even talking with anyone. I knew that I needed to take responsibility for my past and create a different future. That day I got out of the car in a better headspace and mindset than I got into it after that meeting.

How Language Shapes Your Relationships

Clearly, the way you communicate with your family and other loved ones is very different from the way you communicate with your colleagues at work. This includes both the words of affirmation you use and the way you approach hard conversations.

Think about your typical day. Carefully consider for a moment how you communicate with your partner or children during the day. What is the primary function of your communication? Is it to share experiences? Impart information? Are you using words that deepen your relationships or tear them down?

Changes in language shift how you engage with others and how you appreciate each situation.

Years ago, I realized that my communications with my wife had become very information focused. I wasn't using my words to deepen our connection. So now, most mornings, she makes tea and I have a cup of coffee and I talk with her. My words and intent are simple and straightforward:

"Vijju, I want you to know my life would be nothing without you," I tell her. "I want you to know how much having you in my life has allowed me to grow. The way you are, how you take care of me and our family's needs, has given me peace and allowed me to grow and focus on the important things in life. Had you not taken care of yourself, it would've been difficult for me to do what I do. So I want to acknowledge you for taking care of me, and how it has enriched my life."

Acknowledging people is a way of expressing my love. Using language to share and express, to connect and bond, that's a creation.

I've had to have hard conversations with loved ones, as well. When engaging in a hard conversation with someone you love, it is imperative to envision a win-win situation. What is going to be the best outcome for all involved? From there, you must have a willingness to be open to the "dance" in the conversation.

It is also vital to validate and reassure the other person in these conversations. For instance, my mother used to love to complain about things. For me, it was sometimes too much to handle, and that negatively affected our relationship. I saw her words as destroying or tearing someone down; she saw it as venting, which kept her from bottling her emotions inside. We had many hard conversations on this topic; we danced with our words, we fought, and we both lost until the day came when we found a way for both of us to win.

Eventually, when she would get in that space, I would step back and say, "Mom, is it that you don't have anyone else to talk to and you need to complain about something? Okay, I will give you this hour to complain about the things that don't work for you. I can do that for you."

By acknowledging her perspective, I validated and reassured her. By setting a time limit on her complaining, I took care of myself and my needs. This was a win-win that allowed us to continue to have a loving relationship built on open communication until she passed away. When she left this planet, she knew that there was an experience of love and acceptance between mother and son because I shifted how I spoke with and listened to her.

How Language Shapes Organizations

We decide if we are going to hire someone at In Time Tec through the language they use. Skills can be taught, but attitude cannot be. That being said, we listen to the language they use to understand what they are looking for in a job. Does the language they use imply they are open to learning and growing? Does their language imply they are a person who is open to change, or does it imply that they are stuck in their ways? What is their attitude toward life? In these interviews, language helps us decide if hiring this person would be a win-win for both them and us. That is the only condition we hire under, and without language, it would be impossible to figure out if our needs aligned.

Our Most Powerful Conversations Are Often the Most Difficult to Initiate

Language can be used to share experiences. It can be used to share information. And it can be used to create or destroy relationships.

For these reasons, I think about language all the time. I dwell on how I use it in the office to express myself and build my professional relationships at In Time Tec and elsewhere. In fact, I have built our company culture around language of commitment and straightforward communication.

That does not mean I do not have challenging conversations at work — I do. In those conversations, I follow my own advice and try my hardest to find a win-win solution to each situation. It is harder than it sounds to decide what a win for me looks like, versus what a win for another person looks like — and most importantly, committing to our outcome being a win-win or no deal at all.

Standing up for yourself and your beliefs can be difficult. Exhausting. Draining. All of us dread having hard conversations with friends, colleagues, loved ones, and even strangers. That is because it takes emotional energy and strength of spirit to be up front about uncomfortable topics, or to call someone out on their bad behavior, or worse yet, to let someone down.

Technology, most notably the rise of smartphones and texting, has given many of us an easy way out of these tough conversations. Why speak face-to-face when you can text? Or more conveniently yet, why text when you can simply "ghost" someone — that is, never respond to or acknowledge that person again?

While emailing, texting, or ghosting may be the easy way out of having a hard conversation with someone, I would argue that these avoidance tactics do real and lasting damage not only to the person you are avoiding, but to yourself and your personal growth.

Understanding the power of language is vital to your growth as a leader and creator. Similarly, engaging in tough conversations is a necessary part of life and a healthy society. That is because when you avoid having a tough conversation about something — say, perhaps you've noticed a coworker skimming company resources — you are implicitly approving of that behavior. With your silence, you are letting that behavior, and the damage it causes, grow in size and scope.

Let's recall the story I shared in the last chapter about the employee whom I asked not to share any new ideas for six months. While this conversation was hard to initiate, it created a new future for him as a leader in our company. In the same way, the conversation I had with a different employee about losing weight has changed the way she shows up for herself and for others. These conversations may be difficult to initiate, but if you are committed to being others-focused, you will find a way to have the conversations that create a better future.

Using Effective Language to Initiate a Hard Conversation

How do you recognize that you need to have a hard conversation with someone? Thanks to chapter three, "Expressing Your Values," you should have confidently identified your core values, like trust, transparency, integrity, and leadership. When you are in a situation where silence would compromise your values, it is time to speak up.

Knowing when you have to engage in a difficult conversation with someone is just the first step. The second step is seeing that conversation through successfully. Chances are, the reason you consider this conversation difficult is because you hold the other person in esteem and are worried they will have a negative reaction to your words. In reality, there are no difficult conversations. There are just conversations!

I have a few key things for you to keep in mind that would take away the hard or difficult part of any conversation:

1. Your words must be personal.

2. You must be clear on what your end goals are and what you see could get in the way.

3. You must acknowledge the person.

4. You must acknowledge the reality of the situation.

Any difficult conversation will become just a conversation if you follow these steps.

Letting an employee go can be one of the most difficult conversations one might experience as a leader, and yet I have been able to shift it from a difficult conversation to just a conversation. This year we hired someone as a technical account manager. After a few months, it became clear that she was not a great fit for the position. She was a wonderful human being, and yet her experience, expertise, and way of working did not match the project requirements or our company culture. I got on a call with this employee and paid close attention to the language I used. I was careful not to make her wrong in any way. I was clear about how I wanted the information to land on her. I told her we chose to let her move on and her last day would be on Friday, but we would continue to compensate her for the next two months. "The reason we are letting you move on is because your experience and expertise do not match project requirements. There will be other places where it could work better and achieve a win-win."

This conversation wasn't difficult because I never made it about her as a human being; it was simply a misalignment. You can design the conversation. By treating it differently, you can create something rather than destroy something. If I would've thought it was going to be a difficult conversation, I would've been anxious, which would've impacted the way I showed up as a leader during this conversation. But I received this note from her:

> **"** Dear Jeet,
>
> I didn't want to say goodbye without properly thanking you for the amazing opportunity of working at In TIme Tec. It was such a pleasure to see a team working happily and cohesively with involved and caring leadership. Thank you for taking a chance on me and offering not just employment but education. You have created something very special Jeet and I will look back on my time there with much gratitude and fondness. **"**

Remember to look past whatever current problem you're addressing to acknowledge that person's role. Recognize the strengths or unique perspectives they bring to the table. By showing them this respect, you signal that your hard conversation is coming from a place of love, not anger or an attempt to undermine them or their work.

You are having this hard conversation for a reason; something the other person has said or done has conflicted with your values, or could in the near future. By being clear about your needs and goals, you also show the other person exactly where the conflict lies and why this hard conversation is taking place.

Giving others insight into your "why" helps underscore that you are trying to have a respectful but hard conversation about a difficult topic, not instigate a fight. It also helps to seek out a win-win resolution to a hard conversation, which makes any hard conversation just a conversation.

However, sometimes you must have multiple conversations to get to a place that is satisfactory for both parties. When you walk away from a conversation, it's important to first acknowledge that no one did anything wrong.

Sometimes you simply have to hit pause and walk away for a bit. Here are the steps I use to re-engage in a conversation that has been left unresolved:

1. Clean things up; acknowledge that the first conversation did not go well.

2. Describe what you experienced in the conversation, and where you think the sticking point is.

3. Commit to keep dancing in the conversation until both of you come to a win/win, and commit to that win/win (unless it is against your values).

Of course, there are difficult conversations in life that have no win-win outcome. In these instances, it's important to acknowledge that there is nothing wrong with the other person or yourself; it just did not work out. Communicating this in a productive way by saying something like, "Let's part ways and we'll both find someone with whom we can work and express ourselves," is a gracious way to end a hard conversation for which there is no acceptable solution.

That's a way of creating something using language. It may not be the end result you desired, but it is still an acceptable result and one that honors both you and the other party. Expressing and sharing your love and affection with another human being, even when you disagree is part of creation.

Take a look at the table below. The words and phrases on the left are limiting; they leave little to no room for creation. The alternatives on the right are more open and make space for creation to happen.

Instead of this...	Try this...
But	And
Burden	Blessing
Help	Stand
Get out of the way	Empower
Attachment	Commitment
Fault	Responsibility
Right/Wrong	Did/Did not work

Through these examples and in this chapter, you've seen that the power of language is nearly infinite. The beauty is, language is a great equalizer, available to everyone regardless of their social status, income, ethnicity, or gender. Learning to communicate effectively, and with love, with those around you is one of the most precious tools a leader and creator can wield.

Without converting my thoughts into reality by taking action, this book would have not been possible. In Time Tec started as an idea in my head. If I and the other four co-founders did not take action, it wouldn't exist. If you continue to let things start and die in your head, without speaking them into existence, your contribution on this planet will be limited. Do you see just how critical language and action is?

After understanding the power of language and action, the natural next steps are to explore how to commit fully to yourself and others — how to embrace and nurture your inner leader. You will understand what it means to take a stand for someone else, and in doing so, change their life.

SELF-REFLECTION

What kind of language do you use with yourself and others?

_____

_____

_____

_____

_____

_____

What is your language creating or destroying?

_____

_____

_____

_____

_____

_____

What kinds of conversations have you been avoiding?

_____

_____

_____

_____

_____

_____

What can you create by having these conversations?

_____

_____

_____

_____

_____

_____

How to Take a Stand

"

"Strong people stand up for themselves, but stronger people stand up for others." – Unknown

I met my now brother-in-law for the first time in 1988, when I was seventeen and he was thirteen. When my wife and I got married, I was twenty-five. My brother-in-law was in his early twenties and had recently started drinking. Initially, he would just drink in the evenings, but it didn't take long to progress to the point that he was drinking in the morning, afternoon, and evening. In 2002, he began to have issues with his liver. This is when I declared that I was taking a stand for his life.

I flew to India to be with him while he was experiencing these challenges. While I was there, he started to recover and make progress toward a healthier life. Unfortunately, the moment I returned home from India, he started drinking again. I kept asking myself, "What more can I do?" When I moved back to India in 2006 to work for a large corporation, I brought him from the north of India to the south where he stayed with me for about six months. I kept working with him. We had many personal conversations about life and his outlook. His spirits seemed better, but the drinking never stopped. His liver continued to suffer, and even got so bad that he would vomit blood. I kept working with him to find out why he was drinking so much. It wasn't just that he was an alcoholic; he was incomplete about his life and he was drinking to escape that feeling. That's when I found a psychiatrist and enrolled him in rehabilitation. Through his psychiatrist, he was also diagnosed with bipolar disorder.

We have continued to work together to this day. He has gotten his life back. He is now married and has an eight-year-old son and five-year-old daughter. It's still a work in progress for both of us. If he has a breakdown, I will get on a call with him at any time of day, no matter what I am doing. I have done everything in my capacity to take a stand for his life; nothing is off the table. Once, I happened to be in India at a client meeting when he had a breakdown. I finished that meeting at 9 p.m. and took a three-hour ride back to the town where he lived. I took care of him until I had to head back at five o'clock the next morning. Taking care of my brother-in-law is important to me. I took a stand for him.

Think back to the last time you took a stand for someone or something. Maybe it was for yourself, or a coworker, or a stranger in a parking lot. Do you remember how your blood rushed through your chest and your palms tingled? Do you remember the pride you felt for living your convictions?

Taking a stand is an exhilarating experience. However, like all things worth doing well in life, it takes practice. In this chapter, let's explore how to commit to yourself and others, and discuss what it means to take a stand for your, or someone else's, life — to truly become a leader worth following.

You Have the Power to Create a Change on the Planet

You must keep this in mind: Nothing happens on this planet until you say so. By that I do not mean that the entire world is waiting around for you. What I mean is, if you want to see change, you cannot wait for someone else to initiate that change. You must stand up and be the change. You must act. Because nothing was ever accomplished on this planet until someone took a stand, and in doing so, became a creator — someone like you. So why not you?

The path of action is not easy; if it were, everyone would do it.

If you want to create something worthwhile and long-lasting — taking care of your family, starting your own business, making a difference in your community, or even committing to be a change agent for world peace — the path is always challenging. But declaring your intentions is the first step toward making it a reality.

Constraints and Challenges Are Part of Creation

Before you begin your journey, it's important to consider life's limitations. Our every thought and action is limited by some type of constraint; gravity itself is a constraint, as is our very limited time here on this planet. It is important that you acknowledge that you're going to deal with constraints in life, as they are part of creation. Constraints can take many forms:

- People, whose emotions or aspirations may conflict with your own.

- Resources, which may be scarce.

- Time, the universal constraint.

Some of these constraints will be known from the beginning of your creation journey and some may come as a challenge along the way. But if you fail to acknowledge as many constraints as you can, you are making your journey that much harder. Conversely, if you focus too much on how constraints may hinder you, you are not focused on the end goal: creation.

Look at everything holistically and whenever possible, include your constraints in your creation. Embracing the challenges life throws at you will strengthen your mindset and give you a better chance at success.

The alternative, of course, is to walk away from creation. Choosing not to do something is also doing. By consciously not doing something, you are making a choice. What is the choice you want to look back on fifteen or twenty years from now and be proud of?

In 2006, I went back to India so I could gain experience in people management. I had tried everything to get a people management role at the corporation I worked for in the U.S., but they wouldn't give it to me. As an entrepreneur, I was confident that I wanted to have the possibility to create abundance for people. But before starting my entrepreneurial journey, I wanted to get experience in how to lead people, and I hadn't gotten the chance to do so in the U.S. I took an internal transfer inside that company from Boise to Bangalore when my son Jai was six years old and my daughter Jiya was six months old.

Fast forward to 2009 when I started In Time Tec. My initial plan was to stay in India full time. I had taken a stand to build leaders in our company on that side of the world. There was no plan for me to come back to the U.S.

But when Jai was nine years old, he started missing the culture in the U.S. He was born here and went to kindergarten here. I saw a nine-year-old boy who was wearing U.S. military jackets, looking for planes, books, and anything else that reminded him of the U.S. One day we were talking, and he said, "Pappu, I really want to go back to the U.S." I said, "Okay, if that's what you want to do, then let's go back." It was as simple as that. So we came back to the U.S. in 2010 when he was ten years old and in the fourth grade. We packed all of our belongings into eight suitcases and moved into a small apartment in Nampa, Idaho.

I did this because I took a stand for Jai's life and the kind of future I wanted to create for my kids. Jai graduated from UC Berkeley with a computer science degree in just three years.

While taking a stand for my family, I have also taken a stand for In Time Tec. I have pretty much been doing two jobs over the past decade. I get up in the morning around 4:30 or 5 a.m. and catch up on what's happening on the India side of the company, because that responsibility still lies on my shoulders. The two founders on the India side don't have much exposure to the U.S. side, and the two founders on the U.S. side don't have much exposure to the India side. That is where I come in, to bridge the gap. After catching up with the India team, I work out and take a shower, then come to the U.S. office until around 4 p.m. After I finish up my day at the office, I go home and take an hourlong nap so I can be productive for my night shift with the India team up until midnight.

I do this because the original plan was that I would be taking over the India team. That responsibility to build leaders on that side of the world is still mine. For more than a decade, I have been working fifteen or sixteen hours a day.

If you are committed, you can take a stand for more than one creation and find a way to make everything work. When you take a stand, nothing is off the table. I never compromised on the stand I took for In Time Tec, and I also made sure that my family was taken care of and peaceful, joyful, and loving.

How to Take a Stand

You know that in order to create, you need to channel your life into something meaningful. You are not just taking a stand to say you did; you understand it is the best way to expand your impact and contribution in life. You are ready. So how do you begin? Start simply by asking yourself a few questions:

- What are you willing to give your life for?

- What matters to you in life?

- What do you want to achieve?

- What do you want to create?

- What inspires you to act?

- What gets you going in life every day?

- What legacy do you want to leave behind?

Remember: In order to create, you need to set your current life aside to take a stand and forge another path. This stand must be something that matters to you, something so critical that if it doesn't work, if it doesn't happen, if you don't produce it, your life will not be fully complete.

It can vary across the spectrum: family, professional, personal, or public. Perhaps you want to be a community leader or run for office. Perhaps you want to send your kids to college. Whatever it is, it is critical to you and you can articulate why.

Finally, and perhaps most importantly, envision your ideal life playing out. What do you see? Once that ideal future is defined, it's something you can take a stand for. Achieving that is creation, because it is a future that is to come. However, it cannot be realized until you take responsibility for it, own it, and create it.

Now, make a declaration. Do this first for yourself, and then practice articulating it to others.

Everyone has heard of the social rights activist, politician, and philanthropist Nelson Mandela.

He is remembered for several things, but perhaps he is best known for successfully leading the resistance to South Africa's policy of apartheid in the 20th century. Mandela is an international symbol of liberty and equality. He dedicated his life to equality for all. This was his declaration:

I have cherished the ideal of a democratic and free society in which all persons live together in harmony and with equal opportunities. It is an ideal which I hope to live for and to achieve. But if needs be, it is an ideal for which I am prepared to die.

— Nelson Mandela

Despite the South African government responding to these requests with repression and violence, Mandela never gave up.

He was arrested and charged with treason in 1956 after a protest that turned violent. After a trial that lasted five years, Mandela was found not guilty. However, in 1962 he was arrested and sentenced to five years in jail, but ultimately ended up behind bars for twenty-seven years.

While he was in jail, he faced harsh conditions and many barriers that were meant to break his stand, but he refused to give up on equality for all people. When Mandela was released, he appeared before 50,000 people on the balcony of City Hall to thank all of his supporters for encouraging his release. And apartheid did not immediately end when Mandela was released from jail, but he negotiated with President de Klerk for a constitution that allowed majority rule when he was seventy-one years old. This is how apartheid was eventually repealed.

This is what it looks like to unconditionally commit your life to something you have taken a stand for.

Navigating the Mental Pitfalls of Taking a Stand

Taking a stand for something vital, urgent, and worthwhile in this life is not an easy path. You might make mistakes or mess up during your journey. You may experience moments of exhaustion, self-doubt, and perhaps the temptation to quit.

I'm sure even Mandela suffered days in jail when he wished nothing more than to walk away from the constraints others had placed on his freedoms because of the stand he took. In some ways, life would be simpler if we ignored the troubles of the world. However, it would also be worse, wouldn't it?

But feeling bad about anything, or guilty for messing up, or worrying in general about your decisions won't get you anywhere. It certainly won't help you create. You need to retain a laser focus on what you stand for. All of the rest becomes part of a game: tasks to overcome, to "level up." With that kind of mindset, any way of being is allowed; any action is possible.

People are motivated to take a stand for many reasons. Sometimes, it's for a desired outcome (like Mandela). Sometimes, you are taking a stand for a cause, or for personal growth. When you discover your why (or whys) for living — those precious causes and ideas and people worth fighting for — you'll find that taking a stand will motivate you, and even provide comfort, when things get tough.

When Taking a Stand for Yourself:

In these moments, it's important to take a deep breath and focus on regeneration. You cannot heal the world if you yourself are sick, and that includes mental health. If you are taking a stand for yourself, focus on what drives you, your commitments. Above all, cherish yourself.

When Taking a Stand for Others:

If others are your focus, make sure you know the "why" that drives them and repeat it to yourself. Remember that, when you take a stand for others, you will not always be liked. Above all, practice ruthless compassion to those who would try to subvert your stand, and hold them accountable in a loving way.

I want to tell you a story about a stand I took for one of our employee's mothers. Before I met her, she was on depression medication for twenty-five to thirty years. When she was at a difficult time in her life and was dependent on her medication, her daughter, who I have been working with for quite some time, suggested that she come talk with me. This is when I declared that I was taking a stand for her. I was going to do everything I could to keep her off the medication for years to come. I wanted her to be in control of her own life, and I knew it was possible.

Going forward we set up a plan that whenever she was feeling down or something wasn't working for her, she was going to call me and we were going to work through it together. Initially, it took some time to build the foundation where she could experience me taking a stand for her. I would sit down and talk with her and she would tell me about a time that she was feeling down, and then would say, "I was going to call you but I know how busy you are and didn't want to bother you." I wasn't okay with that. I told her that she needs to make the call and I will be the one to decide if I'm too busy or not. I get to decide if I am going to answer her call. I get to make that choice. Of course, I also told her that if I don't answer I will call back shortly after, when I am available. I will always get back to her. That is one of the commitments I made when I took a stand for her. I encourage her to call me whenever she needs, no matter the day and no matter the time.

Now, it doesn't even cross her mind to get back on her medication. She feels free and no longer lets her moods and feelings run the show. She has her life back and yet I still meet with her regularly and I am prepared to be there for her if she has a breakdown. Lately, I see an immense peace and joy in her life, where she is fulfilled inside and able to express her love for her spouse, daughter, and grandkids freely.

How I Practice Taking a Stand

Taking a stand for my employees is one important way I show up for them. In practice, that looks different for every single person. For one employee, taking a stand simply means offering career advice. For others, it can be so much more.

For instance, we were recently hiring for a position. One of my employees came to me and said, "Jeet, a former coworker of mine applied for this job. I'll admit, I actually had to fire her from her last position. However, since then she's dealt with some personal issues and is on a path to being a better person and employee."

So, we interviewed this person. In our interview, she was honest, and that meant being raw and vulnerable and owning her past failings as an employee and as a person. It was a pretty intense interview.

Afterward, I pulled her aside and said, "I don't think your friend is right for this position, but that doesn't mean she isn't right for this company in the future. If you want to take a stand for her, I'll take a stand for you."

She agreed. So we decided that every Friday, as part of her workday, my employee would meet with this former coworker and offer whatever guidance or support she needed. As part of standing up for this person, she also volunteered to pay for her to take a leadership course. And I volunteered to pay for their coffee each week.

I wish that for everyone reading this book. I wish for you the ability to take a stand with passion because until you do so, creation is not possible. And creation is our ultimate goal. That said, we must also be ready to produce and measure our results.

You can clearly see how beautiful life can be when you are constantly creating, and how to make the most of your life as a creator by measuring the impact your work has on the world.

Remember: the ultimate goal of taking a stand is creation. If you won't take a stand to create a better planet, then who will?

••• SELF-REFLECTION •••

Name a time when *you* have taken a stand for someone. How did that feel?

_____
_____
_____
_____
_____
_____

Name a time when *someone* took a stand for you. How did that feel?

_____
_____
_____
_____
_____
_____

Does it feel better to take a stand or have someone take a stand for you?

_____
_____
_____

Think of something you can create. Who can you enroll in being a stand for you in that creation? Have that conversation.

_____
_____
_____
_____
_____
_____

CELEBRATE
Part 3

Results Are Key to Creation

> **"The results of your life reflect the standards you've set."**
> – Robin Sharma

For the last ten chapters of this book, you have committed to change. Not only for a better you, but for a better world. You have written down your values, run through tough conversations in your head and explored what it means to take a stand for something or someone.

Change is never easy; I want to recognize your efforts to commit to this hard and rewarding path. You are now ready for the real work to begin: producing results in creation. What creation looks like to each one of us is very personal, because it is literally the formation of something that wouldn't have been possible without you.

For me, one act of creation was starting my own company. For years, I worked hard to make it happen. However, I soon realized that simply starting a company was not enough. In fact, starting a company was the easy part. My creation was building a successful company full of happy, healthy employees who felt empowered to grow and reach their full potential.

You are probably rolling your eyes and thinking, "But Jeet, of course your employees will tell you that they are happy at their jobs; you're their boss. They could be lying."

I understand your point. It's impossible to know if creation was successful if I cannot measure the results to see if I've created an impact. That is why so many businesses are concerned with profit margins, quarterly numbers, and cost structures. Numbers are easy to point to and say, "Look at how successful we are!" or "Our profits are down, we are less successful than last year."

Employee happiness may be harder to quantify, but the key here is that I knew right away that I must figure out a way to do it. Happy employees are the heart of my creation. If you do not take the time to measure the results of your creation, you will never know if it has been successful.

For example, if I commit to financially supporting my daughter through college but never follow up to see if she's going to class, has my creation been successful? If, after I got married, I stopped telling my wife I love and appreciate her, or checking in with her to see if she still loves and appreciates me, is our creation successful?

You cannot call your creation successful if you do not measure the results, because you do not know if you've created an impact. Perhaps more importantly, you cannot celebrate your successes if you never acknowledge them. And without acknowledging your creation and its impact, and celebrating both, how do you move on to your next creation?

How do you ensure that creation becomes as natural to you as breathing?

Creation as a Way of Life

My goal with this book is to get you so comfortable with being a creator that it becomes your lifestyle. It is simply who you are. So let's talk about the steps you need to get there.

To be a successful creator, you must be able and willing to answer these four questions:

- What are you creating?

_____

_____

- Why are you creating?

_____

_____

- How are you going to create it?

_____

_____

- When do you know it has been done?

_____

_____

The "what" should be informed by your personal strengths and interests. The "why" should be aligned with your values. The "how" will be the steps you take to get there. So that just leaves figuring out how you know when you've achieved your goal.

Chances are, your creation will be ambitious. It will not be the sort of thing that can be achieved in one day, so you must set milestones for yourself to help keep you motivated and measure your progress. These milestones should be granular and time sensitive.

For instance, if my creation is supporting my daughter until she is a successful college graduate, here would be my milestones, or my "how":

- Make an agreement with her that I will pay for her tuition, room and board as long as she is committed to her studies and gets good grades.

- Check in with her before the beginning of each semester to understand what classes she's taking and how they relate to her chosen major.

- Call her at least once a week to offer her emotional support and listen to any struggles she has, and to ensure she's happy.

- If she is feeling unsure about her major, talk her through how she envisions her future, what career would make her happiest, and what major might best support that future.

- Visit her at least once every semester to participate in her campus life.

- Check in with her before finals week to see what she needs from me in terms of support.

- Check in with her at the end of the semester to see how her grades were.

- Re-evaluate my milestones as necessary based on feedback I get from her.

You'll notice that many of these milestones involve simply showing up for my daughter — being there in whatever capacity she needs me to be. These are easy milestones to celebrate. Time-sensitive milestones revolve around the traditional college calendar. Values milestones revolve around my desire to ensure she is not wasting the precious opportunity that college affords by slacking on her studies. Values milestones also include me taking a stand for my daughter and ensuring she can use her education to plan for the future she desires.

If we do not reach a milestone — for instance, if she gets a bad grade in a class — does that mean my creation is a failure? No. It simply means that we need to evaluate that milestone and why it wasn't reached, and what we need to do to ensure we reach it next semester.

Do you see how different that looks from the goal to simply "get my kid through college?" That vague goal does not address whether or not your child thrives in school, or even if they graduate. There is no joy in that goal, no caring, and the only milestone is the end of school — which could mean that your child drops out.

By being deliberate in setting my goal and detailed in setting my milestones, I am holding myself (and my daughter) accountable to our creation. I am hopefully taking some of the stress and pressure of such a large financial and life-changing decision off of both of us by breaking that yearlong goal down into manageable chunks.

Each semester, she moves the needle. Each semester, we have the chance to make progress, evaluate the results, and then celebrate.

How to Measure Results

We measure results because they are the tangible conversion of your intentions into reality. You are not creating an impact until you start producing results. As you may have noticed in my previous example of my daughter's education, results don't have to be oriented around you; they can, and should, involve others.

Results for others can mean standing for someone else and tracking how they meet milestones. This follow-through works well with family, work colleagues — there is no limit.

Remember my desire to create a successful company full of happy, healthy employees who felt empowered to grow and reach their full potential? Some of my milestones were common sense: company growth and employee retention, for example. Others were more abstract. I began to gauge the health and growth of our employees through our interactions. Sure, people will tell you what you want to hear ... at first. They will tell you that they're happy. But over time, I built a culture of trust and openness for my employees. They saw that I stood for them. Because of this, they began coming to me with their challenges.

This was a huge milestone for me: Being a leader that employees trusted enough to seek for advice when they have challenges or problems. Not just professional challenges, but personal ones as well.

It may seem counterintuitive to measure a milestone by how comfortable your employees feel sharing their challenges, but that's exactly what I did.

Through my efforts, I created and led a business that, for six consecutive years, was one of the fastest growing companies in America. It was also voted one of the best places to work in Idaho for five years in a row. I wasn't born in America and didn't live in Idaho up until twenty-three years ago, yet I had the ability to transform hundreds of lives through my creation. Now do you understand the full power of creation?

Money as a Factor in Creation

I've always said that money is required to live, but love is the reason to live. And while money is not the reason to live, it is the fuel that powers life. Money alone will never be enough, but the conversation around money can be shifted once you define what kind of money you need. You will know the answer to that question once you define what kind of life you want to live on this planet. In order to produce results, you must first know what your goals are. Ask yourself:

• What kind of car do I want to drive?

• What kind of neighborhood do I want to be a part of?

• What kind of house do I want to live in?

• Do I want to put my kids through college, and pay for it?

• By what age do I want to be financially free?

All of these answers will be different depending on what you prioritize. For example, I ask myself, what kind of car would be a nice car for me and why? I personally think of a nice car as something comfortable and safe for me to commute in. That's why I still drive a 2010 Lexus with 123,000 miles on it. My car works great, and it never crosses my mind to upgrade my car, even though I can.

Similarly, my house is a 2006 build that I bought in 2011, and again, I have no plans to change it even though I can afford to do so. For me, sending both my kids to college is critical. Not only sending them to college, but them being debt-free when they graduate.

If you are currently struggling with money, look at your bank account. Ask yourself: What would be a good amount to currently have in your bank account at this age? Then ask yourself, what amount of money do you want to have in your bank account five years from now? Now that you know your financial goal based on your priorities, responsibilities, and commitment to live the type of life you want to live, what do you need to do to get there? How much of each paycheck do you need to set aside? Once you set these goals, it's important to track your results along the way.

The goal of money is to be financially free. How do you know when you are financially free? It starts by first defining what financially free means, which can be different for everyone. Create a roadmap for yourself, and keep in mind that your end result may change in the future as your priorities shift. For me, I made a declaration to be debt-free and have enough money to comfortably retire by the age of 50.

I knew I wanted to achieve this, so I decided I would never take on debt I knew I would not be able to repay.

However, for my younger sister's wedding, I found myself in debt before I knew it. You see, since my father had passed away and I was the only male in the family, it was my responsibility to pay for my sister's wedding when she was 21 years old. This was a debt I could not avoid because I wanted to make sure my sister got married properly and was treated the same way my three older sisters were. It was a priority for me. For her wedding, I borrowed money from my friends and relatives. I was also accumulating debt from the college I was attending during this time and was financially responsible for taking care of my mom.

When I got my first job at the age of twenty-five, I set aside a portion of every paycheck because my primary focus was to pay off that debt. Since I knew I had the financial responsibility of my own family, my mom, and the debt accumulated from my schooling and my sister's wedding, I knew I would have to be patient. As you can see, the odds were stacked against me in every way possible. I went from a young boy with no money and so many responsibilities, starting adulthood with debt and no access to money, to being financially free by age 50 and having enough money in the bank to retire comfortably and send my two kids to college. Can you see how important these results are to me?

There is a saying I have heard: "Being born poor is a curse, dying poor is laziness." And while everyone reading this will be at different points on their own journey to financial freedom, I have some advice for all of you to make money less of a burden:

• Be mindful and thoughtful about your money. When I moved to America, I bought a small Honda Civic and lived in a small apartment even though my wife and I had two children. We did this because we knew that in order to create the life we wanted, we had to make intentional financial choices.

• No matter how much you are earning, you can save. Even if it is only a dollar a day. It might seem impossible some days when faced with so many money decisions. But every little bit counts.

• Be patient. Wealth is not created in a year.

• Do not underestimate how much money runs your life. It can be evil or it can be a blessing. Be responsible about it.

Time as a Factor in Creation

There is a delicate balancing act to creation. On one hand, you must be patient, because creation takes time and may include setbacks. On the other hand, you must know when to gauge if a creation is taking up too much of your time. The more time that is required, the more you are taking away from your impact.

For instance, imagine if it takes my daughter ten years of full-time school to finish her undergraduate degree because she keeps switching majors. Of course, I will still be proud of her, but do you see how the impact of my creation of supporting her through that process has been lessened?

At some point in that process, I would probably have to reevaluate how my financial support might be hindering her progress. Perhaps I've made it too comfortable to be in school; perhaps she is afraid of graduating and moving on to that next step in her life. If that were the case, I would have to walk away from that creation and let her own it completely. I could do this while still standing for her and supporting her emotionally.

In this way, evaluating our milestones helps us know when we are not having our desired impact. It gives us the peace of mind to know we've done everything we can to ensure our creation is a success, while also acknowledging that some things are out of our control. It gives us the space to launch new creations without feeling like a failure.

Results in Health and Fitness

It was 1999 when I came to America. I had a bad habit of eating unhealthy and processed foods. One day I woke up and my chest hurt. I thought to myself, what's the problem here? I was 5'8" and 198 pounds. Honestly, I hadn't even recognized that I was overweight at the time. Because my father had passed away from likely heart problems at a similar age, I went to the doctor and had my bloodwork done. Everything came back normal, besides the health of my heart. The doctor shared that if I continued living the same way, I would be in a difficult place in ten years. I knew that if I wanted to be around for my kids, I had to do something about my health. Initially, I cut out all high-fat foods from my diet. I went from full-fat milk to skim milk. No more butter. I reduced sugar and cut deep fried foods out of my diet. I knew that changing my diet alone was not going to be enough; I needed to exercise too. When I initially started exercising, I couldn't even walk for half a mile because my cardiovascular health was so weak.

Your body is your home, and if your home is in disarray, how can you fully show up for others? I consistently and constantly worked on my health and fitness and celebrated hitting every milestone along the way. I was, and still am, committed to never going back to my old eating habits. My weight slowly started to taper off and I am 150-155 pounds today. My BMI remains at a healthy level and I work out every day, intermittently fast, and watch what I eat. My goal is to sustain these habits for the rest of my life. I still socially drink when I go out with my friends, because I've found the importance that balance plays in this aspect of my life.

Once a year on the week of my birthday, I go to my doctor for my yearly health checkup and bloodwork. I also weigh myself once a week to ensure I am still in the 150-155-pound range. If I find that I am over 155 pounds, I tighten everything up until I am back at or under 155 pounds. I also pay close attention to my pant size. My goal is to stay at thirty-thirty. The moment my waist size becomes thirty-one, I know it's time to tighten my eating and exercise habits. I pay close attention to all of this because it is how I measure my results. And as we discussed earlier in the chapter, how do you consider your creation successful if you do not measure the results?

It's important to note that there is a distinction between health and fitness. One can be healthy and not fit, and one can be fit and not healthy. I have made a declaration to be both.

Because of these structures I have set up in my life, when I go on stage or in front of groups of people, I am both confident and comfortable. I am clear that how I feel impacts how I present myself and present our company. If I show up as someone who is physically unfit, one of the messages I am communicating is that I am unable to take care of myself. And if I can't take care of myself, how am I going to take care of the larger responsibilities that I have on my shoulders?

I am not a health and fitness expert, but I have learned a few things about staying healthy.

- Don't misuse your body. A few years ago, I had to have shoulder surgery because I had been pushing my body to do things that were harmful. I have since learned to listen to my body and respect its capabilities.

- Health is from the inside. It is the stats that doctors look at. Fitness is how you feel. Do you feel comfortable and confident? Are you unrestricted by your body to create the life you want?

- Get your yearly checkups. Do not skip wellness exams. They are imperative to live a long, healthy, happy life.

- Do not be overly restrictive with your diet. Have fun and adapt to your lifestyle.

- Vary your workouts and be mindful of your body's capacity to move.

- Make it a family affair! My family has a group gym membership and we go every Saturday together. We share our Apple Watch statistics and make It a point to close all of our rings together.

- Your body is your temple. It goes wherever you go. It dies, you die. Honor it.

What if Your Creation Is Unsuccessful?

Let me be clear: No one in life is a perfect example of success. If you think you know of one such example, either you have not been paying close enough attention or they are masters at deception.

Despite your best intentions and efforts, you may not be able to achieve desired results. You may launch a business that fails. You may put one-hundred percent into a relationship and only get twenty-five percent back. You may take a stand for someone who ultimately refuses to stand for themselves.

What do you do?

- You reflect on what went wrong.

- Figure out what was missing.

- Try again or make a new commitment to a new creation.

I want to touch on that last point for a second, because this decision will rely on you sticking to your values and following your intuition. For example, if your new restaurant failed because you launched it the month before a global pandemic began, it is worth trying again once the pandemic has subsided.

Conversely, perhaps you gave one-hundred percent to a friendship in which you were treated poorly in return. After you walk away from the friendship, your friend vows to change in order to save the friendship. Of course, you can listen to their promises to make changes. If you decide to continue this friendship, I would encourage you to outline specific milestones that ensure you are being fully loved and supported this time around. But you could also just decide that the creation did not work out and it is time for you to put your energy into a new one.

I caution you to always remember that, like all things in life, time is of the essence. Life often throws us detours that we must adapt to and even embrace. However, if a creation is taking too much time, if meeting your milestones is stretching further and further out of your reach, it is diluting your ability to launch new creations and take new stands. Just as there is strength in creating, there is strength in acknowledging when to walk away.

Remember to Celebrate Your Creations, No Matter How Small or Challenging

Sometimes when we complete a creation, there is a sense of loss or mourning that accompanies it. This makes sense: you have been on a journey with this creation for a great while and that journey has now come to an end. Every ending in our life, however small, brings with it a little sorrow.

Other times, a creation can be imposed on you, like my sister's wedding was. Or perhaps your employer has tasked you with creating a new program, and the task doesn't align with your skill set or spark enthusiasm. When that happens, you may feel a sense of relief and a desire to forget about the creation as quickly as possible and move on with your life.

Whatever the case may be, it's important that you acknowledge and celebrate each milestone and small success during your journey of creation. Find the joy in the celebration! You did it! You saw it through to completion–through all the hard work and setbacks and reluctancies. There is happiness to be found there. Creation without celebration is a slight to your hard work, your talents, and the creation itself.

If you cannot celebrate what was created in an authentic way, celebrate your intentions for trying to create. Celebrate the catalyst behind this creation; if it was a project your boss put on your plate, know that you've proven yourself a competent, enthusiastic employee. Celebrate taking a stand for it and following through. Celebrate the opportunities it may open up for you. Or simply celebrate your ability to give your life to something so completely.

You see, celebrating each of your creations is vital to acknowledging your greatness. When a focus on creation becomes your lifestyle, you will find yourself leaning into action more and more each day. Your life will be challenging and vitalizing. You will create abundance and, through it, come to recognize and fully embrace your importance on this planet.

"The secret of getting things done is to act."

— Dante Alighieri

SELF-REFLECTION

What results have you produced that you feel proud of so far?

What results have you seen from doing the exercises in this book?

What other results would you still like to produce? What actions do you need to take to achieve more results?

Connect with Your Greatness

"Never underestimate the power of dreams and the influence of the human spirit. We are all the same in this notion: The potential for greatness lives within each of us."
– Wilma Rudolph

If you have made it this far in this book without stopping to acknowledge how great you are, how truly magnificent your ideas and aspirations are, and how deeply your potential for creation runs, please do so now. And if you are still unsure of your own capacity for greatness, I suggest flipping to the beginning of this book, but instead of reading it to yourself, this time, try shouting it out loud.

Because you are filled with greatness. Some of it is out in the world; some of it is untapped and waiting to be released. In this chapter, we will review how to connect with your untapped greatness. What makes your greatness unique is that it is purely yours. Your capacity for creation is uniquely yours, as well.

Earth is estimated to be about 4.5 billion years old. As human beings, we each have our own little slice of life to experience. This planet was here before you and I showed up and it will continue to be here way after we are gone. So why are we here? It is our God-given purpose, our birthright, to experience this life to the fullest. And yet, there is still so much suffering and there are so many challenges. One of the ways to overcome these is to connect with your greatness. This not only helps you to find that peace, joy, and happiness for yourself, but it also helps you create possibilities for others. Connecting with your greatness is the only way to live your life and experience it to the fullest. It's your choice. Do you want to simply survive on this planet? Or do you want to thrive on this planet?

Look at me, for example. Someone else could have founded In Time Tec; indeed, other global software solutions companies exist. A large part of being a creator is seeing a need in the world and filling it with your skills, passion, and expertise.

But no one else could have brought together the same collection of people to help me found this company. And no one else could have grown their company around the set of values and principles that I have. And indeed, if you visit other global software solutions companies, you may or may not see their employees taking midday breaks to work out together, or approaching their managers for mentoring advice, or being encouraged to take leadership seminars or to get emotional support for their personal problems.

In Time Tec is anchored in my values, and it is powered by my belief that all employees should be supported and mentored to reach their highest personal potential. Because I am the source of this company, no one else could have created it in the way that I have done. It is an extension of me.

That is what I mean when I speak of connecting to your greatness. There are ideas, relationships, companies — things that exist only in your mind right now as wants or wishes, that only you can create. They are not possible without you and they will never come to be until you spark life into them.

How to Be Present to Your Greatness

I still remember the day I felt connected with my greatness for the first time. I finally believed that I could make things happen. There was a cricket tournament in my village, and we invited fifteen other cricket teams from the surrounding villages. We first figured out what it was going to take to put together a successful tournament. Since my team was hosting the tournament, we needed to raise money. After school, my teammates and I would go collect money. In those days it cost around $80-$100 to run a tournament. That may not sound like much, but when the average donation ranges from one cent to five cents, you can imagine how many doors we needed to knock on. We also needed to put together the bracket, prepare the field, and plan meals and lodging arrangements for the visiting teams. I was one of the leaders for these responsibilities, not by designation, but by design. I took on this leadership role because I was so taken by the creation of this tournament.

The day before the semi-finals and finals it was pouring. I still vividly remember how disappointed I was. The next morning, when it finally stopped raining, the field was drenched. I worked with some of my teammates to get sand to dry the field because there were still four teams left in the tournament. When the tournament resumed, I led our team to reach the finals and later on win the championship game. I made about sixty of our teams' eighty runs that day and was awarded MVP of the entire tournament. I connected with my greatness and made sure our team won the championship. When we received the trophy that day, the whole town was there to support us. This was the first time in my life when I really felt like I could do big things.

As I have mentioned in previous chapters, you were designed to be great; it is a possibility that resides within you. Every child that is born on this planet comes with this possibility because every human being is born the same way. You cannot look at a small child and say, "He is going to be a Nelson Mandela. Or a Martin Luther King. Or a Mother Teresa."

Being great is more than just being born; it means doing great things with your life. There is also the possibility that you will never connect with your greatness. That is a choice only you can make. Ignoring your greatness is a waste of humanity. Think of the wasted life, the loss of creation, of contribution, of impact, of making this whole world a better place to live. That is all lost when you choose to stick with the status quo.

The people in this life who become extraordinary are ordinary people who made the choice to go above and beyond. No one gave it to them. They accepted their greatness and connected to the possibilities that greatness allowed for them. This allowed them to create.

I connected to my greatness when I finally accepted myself. Once I was peaceful, happy, joyful, healthy, I started asking myself searching questions. I kept saying to myself, "There must be more in life."

To connect with your greatness, ask yourself these questions:

• Why am I living on this planet? *You can let life live you, or you can use your life to create an impact.*

_____

_____

_____

_____

• Twenty years from now, what will I regret not accomplishing? *Your creation must align with your passions and values. This means you can truly devote your energy to creation.*

_____

_____

_____

_____

• Who in my life needs to be awakened to their own greatness? Who can I take a stand for?

_____

_____

_____

_____

You can ask yourself these questions in order to connect to your greatness, or after you connect to your greatness. Both are beneficial. The first way helps you take a stand for your own life;

the second helps you expand beyond it. It's important to nurture yourself and surround yourself with people who can lovingly push you to do more.

When you connect with your greatness, it can feel overwhelming. Emotions arise because you are committing to something you care deeply about; you are investing in yourself and your dreams. Don't forget that realizing these dreams can take time. It's okay to take baby steps toward your dreams.

If you are having trouble connecting with your greatness, or if you just aren't sure what your greatness may be, I need you to first ingrain this in your head:

❝❞

You are destined for greatness. We are all destined for greatness. It is our birthright.

You need to believe and accept this. It is the first step.

Now ask Yourself: Am I Ready to Be a Creator?

Creation is compelling. As you've considered your potential for greatness, you've likely thought about the things in life that compel you — your aspirations. Creation is the formation of something that wouldn't be possible without you, something new that allows you to impact the world or, on a smaller scale, the people in it.

Yet, being awakened to your potential for greatness is different from embracing creation. There are personal criteria you must consider before embarking on such a journey.

In essence, creation makes life worth living. But to first establish that you're in a place to be a creator, you must revisit the lessons learned in chapter three, "Identifying Your Needs." Now is the time to check in with those needs, because you cannot create for others if your basic needs are unfulfilled. Ask yourself:

- Do I have enough money to take care of my needs? Do I regularly worry about my finances?

- Am I physically and mentally healthy? Am I emotionally strong? Do I have confidence that I can live my life without pressing physical, mental, or emotional constraints?

- Do I have the relationships that matter? Are they whole, complete, and stable?

- Do I have a circle of support from family and friends that I can rely on if I need support for my creation?

If the answer to each of these questions is "yes," you are ready to create.

If the answer is no, be patient with yourself. Most human beings who feel stuck never take the steps to become unstuck. This is because they refuse to acknowledge what they need or when to say no and take care of themselves first.

Without having enough in your own life to feel healthy and happy, how can you be expected to give yourself to others?

In my case, I always wanted to be an entrepreneur. I was taken by the fact that I could make life better for me and better for others. However, I didn't have the money. And I knew I wanted to make enough money to take care of my family's needs before I embarked on my entrepreneurial journey.

In December of 2004, I made a small investment with my buddy and In Time Tec co-founder Sandeep. It wasn't until five years later that we started In Time Tec.

This was because I wanted to make sure I saved money for four or five more years before starting a business. I wanted to make sure that In Time Tec became what it is today, but still have enough money to take care of my family in case it didn't. I was inspired and driven, but not naive.

I also took steps to ensure I was both physically and mentally fit to be a business owner. I worked out regularly, read books, and attended seminars to make sure I was ready. I made sure that my wife was on board and that starting a business would not negatively impact our family. I built strong relationships with the other co-founders to make sure we kicked off our business on a strong footing.

My point is, the majority of us have responsibilities we need to take care of first in order to successfully create. In my case, I wanted to make sure that we created a stable platform that could launch successfully.

This creation took years. Patience and preparation are key to creating something great. You cannot build something big overnight. It takes time to build a foundation that will last.

Keep in mind that creation doesn't have to mean starting a company or writing a book. It could be volunteering your time or money to a cause, losing weight, becoming a foster parent, or even helping teach children.

The key is that you must know what your dreams are and do whatever it takes to pursue those dreams.

One of our employees, Jennifer, connected with her greatness when she agreed to start volunteering at her church in the early mornings teaching children. Although early mornings aren't her thing, Jennifer knew the difference she could make in these children's lives and connected with her greatness. She approaches teaching from a stance of curiosity, love, and support. Kids aren't always used to having someone they can count on to operate from a place of love, so you can imagine the impact this has.

What inspires me about Jennifer's story is her commitment to creation and her ability to go beyond her moods and feelings. While she works a full-time job and takes care of her family, she still does what she loves and connects with her greatness. Again, you don't have to start a company or write a book to connect with your greatness; greatness can happen anywhere.

Another employee, Justin, connected with his greatness when he decided he no longer wanted to be overweight. He set up a structure in his own life to start working out every day and eat healthier.

What inspires me about Justin's story is that he was so taken with the difference that health and fitness made in his own life that he wanted to help others discover it for themselves. He became the lead trainer and co-owner of a local gym in order to help others take control of their lives — to connect with their greatness. Even after changing his career to the software industry, he still continues to help others. He volunteers his time to coach strength training for a local high school mountain bike racing team, creates workout plans for friends, and meets with In Time Tec team members from across the globe as a source of accountability and inspiration.

How to Identify What You Want to Create

When you are ready to connect with your greatness and start creating, it is time to once again consider what you learned in chapter three, "Express Your Values." What motivates you? What makes life worth living? What skills and talents do you bring into this world that are uniquely your own?

If you are still having trouble envisioning your creation, ask yourself these questions:

- How can I bring love into action?

- How can I take a deeper interest in other human beings' lives?

- There is so much suffering in the world, how can I relieve some of it?

In order to be both a leader and creator, you need to know what you are doing and why you are doing it. You must be an expert. You must speak the truth, because otherwise, people can hear your inauthenticity and they won't follow you.

Through these questions, you can start narrowing down your creation. Remember that you don't have to build buildings in order to be a creator. Your creation could be as simple as creating an impact in one human being's life. That can mean helping someone else wake up to their own greatness, or even taking care of yourself. There are more than eight billion people living on this planet. If we were all taking care of ourselves, this world would be a very different place to live. That's an invitation. Once you've taken care of yourself, you can go beyond yourself.

Bringing Creation to Fruition

Once you have settled on a creation, remember that the path forward is not always linear — or fast. You must commit to yourself each day, and in doing so, commit to your creation. For this reason, daily rituals — ideally, morning and night — are vital. It doesn't have to take long, however, it is important that you remain focused. This will allow you to be fully present and deliberate and invest in each conversation without distraction throughout your day.

During your daily rituals, step away from distractions like cell phones, email, even television. Now, take a few deep breaths and ask yourself:

- Am I complete?

- Am I healthy?

- Do I have what I need to create?

- Am I mentally ready to create?

If you answer no to any of these questions, do not beat yourself up. Give yourself grace, time, and even space if you must. These daily check-ins allow you to course-correct on a small scale, ensuring that you do not fail on a large scale.

Lastly, in addition to your daily check-ins, it's important to periodically check in with your calendar and audit your time, as well as your creation's progress. Ask yourself:

- Where is your time going?

- What kinds of things are you involved in?

- Are you stretching beyond yourself?

- Are you maintaining the status quo or are you working on creating new things?

- Are you making progress? Why or why not?

Remember, there is a difference between walking away from something because you are not creating an impact or making a difference and giving up because it's too hard.

In the grand scheme of things, these questions will help you shift your life closer to creation.

For me, this book is a creation, and it has taken years to create. I have long had the seeds of this book inside me. I have yearned to be able to share my knowledge with others who want to move beyond themselves and give back to their communities and the people they love — to become creators.

Yet for me, there was no question that this book would get written. That is because, for me, creation is not work. It is a way of living. If I don't do this, I cannot sleep peacefully. I will have no peace of mind.

I had to balance this yearning to create with the practicalities of my already busy life: being a healthy, centered person; being a loving, attentive husband; being present for my children; being a leader for my business; and standing for my employees.

You can see how this project may have felt overwhelming at times. You can understand how it took years to create. And yet, by following the steps I outlined above, I was able to create it. And by following these same steps, you can successfully create, as well.

After creation is perhaps the most important step in all of this: **celebrating your creation, celebrating your life!**

"Greatness begins beyond your comfort zone.

— Robin S. Sharma

SELF-REFLECTION

Who do you admire for their greatness? What does it look like in action?

_____

_____

_____

_____

_____

_____

How would you define your greatness?

_____

_____

_____

_____

_____

What do you want to create through your greatness? What possibilities
do you see?

_____

_____

_____

_____

13 Celebrate Life

> "The more you praise and celebrate your life, the more there is in life to celebrate." – Oprah Winfrey

In my experience, feelings have flavors just as powerful as some foods. Nothing tastes quite as bitter as regret, just as not even the ripest mango tastes quite as sweet as celebration. For better or for worse, these powerful flavors linger long after the events that inspired them.

Recall the tongue-curling sourness of being caught in a lie by someone you admire. Now think about the flush of sweetness that swept through you the first time you were recognized for a job well done. We cannot escape life without regrets. Indeed, without making mistakes and regretting them, we would never have the opportunity to learn, grow, and succeed.

However, this book is ultimately about helping you minimize your regrets and what-ifs, and celebrate the sweetness of life on a daily basis. It is my hope that this book will help you know yourself with a strength of conviction you never thought possible, and through that self-knowledge, you will have the tools to become a creator. A leader. A world changer.

Throughout these chapters, you have made great strides in becoming that creator. We have now reached the final and most joyous step: celebration. Because creation without celebration is not living.

Celebration sounds easy, but it is not always so. This chapter will walk you through why celebrating not only your creations, but life, in general, is so important. It will also give you the tools you need to cope when doubts arise, tragedy strikes, and you don't feel like celebrating.

Celebration Is Personal

Every day, just as I take time to check in with myself and my goals and needs, I also take a moment to celebrate how much my life is filled with creation. I see it in my home, with my wife and two kids, and our extended family. I see it in my work, with employees on two continents that I have hired and mentored, with clients and partners whom I have built meaningful and lasting relationships with.

To think that a fatherless boy from a poor family could accomplish so much still sometimes amazes me. It also fills me with hope, because if I could climb so far from my humble beginnings, then it proves that everyone can change the circumstances of their lives at any time.

Celebrating is important because it helps you to take a step back from the rat race that we call life, ignore the noise of day-to-day life, and acknowledge the positive changes you're making on this planet. It requires honoring the hard work you have put into your creations. Celebrating allows you to step back and recognize your greatness.

Celebration is so very vital because life is messy and it can get overwhelming, especially if you're ambitious. Life can feel like a never-ending mountain, as some of our creations never end. You will never stop parenting your children, for example. Yet if we take the time to stop and joyously acknowledge our creations, we are recognizing that even this never-ending mountain has peaks with incredible views if we give ourselves the time and grace to stop and admire them.

All Parts of Life Are Worthy of Celebration

When you embrace the life of a creator, the world opens up to you. Yet the psychology of human beings remains always at play around you, including the idea that ignorance is bliss. The idea that we cannot change our fate. The myth that some people are simply born for greatness. While you may not believe these things, others around you will. And it will cause them to shrug their shoulders and give up or, worse yet, not begin any grand creations at all.

During hard times, it may be tempting to lean on these myths as well. But to do so is to ignore a vital part of living.

The truth is, life is not predetermined; it is full of choice. Here is another truth: Life is not always fair. Despite your best efforts and intentions, you may experience terrible loss in your life. You might fail an exam. You may get fired from your job. Your beloved business may go bankrupt. Your marriage may fail. You might lose a loved one. That is because we cannot live our lives in a bubble; life is not bound to our whims and wishes. Bad things will happen to us.

A key part of celebrating life is acknowledging these hard truths. In celebrating life, you are not only celebrating creation, you are celebrating choice. By that, I do not mean the choice to fail, but the choice to accept life as it comes, both good and not so good.

When you learn to wholly embrace and celebrate life, including your personal failures and everything outside of your control, you will find yourself in a state of permanent celebration. Each day, the list of things you privately celebrate will grow and change, and in doing so, you'll be able to look beyond the peaks and valleys of your successes and failures to see the stunning vista spread below you. This is an example of life in celebration. This is how life is designed to be lived.

How to Stay Present and Own Your Power

Just as we know that tragedy is a natural part of life, it is also natural to have doubts or questions when not so good things happen in your life. You may find yourself wondering, "What's the purpose of all this? What's the goal of living?"

What I have learned about life is that its purpose revolves around these three things: time to spend, choices to make, and moments to celebrate.

Your power lies in remembering these three things and letting them center you when you feel lost.

You see, being born is not anyone's choice, just as most people won't choose when they leave this planet. Between life and death we're given precious little time and nearly infinite possibilities for how to use it. Time doesn't stop, it doesn't go backward or forward, you cannot create it or destroy it. It moves at its own pace.

Those who are truly centered in themselves and at peace with their lives are aware of the preciousness of time. They do not waste it wallowing in the past, or daydreaming (too much) into the future. They use their time to make choices, because everything is a choice. That is the power of being human. Even choosing to do nothing is a choice.

Yet whatever actions you take in this life, the outcomes are beyond your control. That is another prickly part of life. The experiences you take from life are shaped by how you handle all that life throws at you. You can fight life, or you can celebrate it.

And let me ask you, why fight what is beyond your control? Why fight when you can spend your energy in discovery, in exploration, in creation, in celebration of all that life has to offer?

Even as you read this, life is happening all around you. It is your choice to see it as a burden, as outside of your control, or to see it as full of possibilities, each worthy of celebration. It is my job within these pages to remind you to make your life count. This planet has been here long before you and me. It will continue long after us. We have this small, precious slice of life to enjoy and celebrate. If we don't, it's a loss. It is a waste.

Given all of that, who has time for resentments? Who has time for grudges when you could be out in the world, creating and leaving your mark?

Let me tell you something: If I died today, I would die content. I truly have no regrets. My life is fulfilled. That is the power of fully embracing and celebrating life. I have learned that life is bliss.

The evaluation and exploration I have urged you to embrace throughout this book reminds us that life is fun. It helps you learn to celebrate life as a choice. It lifts you from a place of ignorant bliss, of thinking "This is just how life is, it's how life's always been, and it's how life has been given to me."

Instead, it is my sincere hope that you walk away from this book knowing that life is full of choices and abundance. And that by committing to yourself, finding yourself, and knowing yourself, you're figuring out what your life should be about. In doing so, you are making your life a permanent celebration.

Because life is available as-is. Not as a compromise, but as a choice. Not as a burden, but as a celebration. You have an opportunity to create a mark, leave a mark, and create an impact. Accept it, celebrate it.

"I love you and there is nothing you can do about it."

Parting words from Jeet

SELF-REFLECTION

What are one to three things you have learned from this book?

_____

_____

_____

_____

_____

_____

How would you like to celebrate your successes and with whom?

_____

_____

_____

_____

_____

_____

What would you tell your past self about your future?

_____

_____

_____

_____

_____

_____

Endnotes

1　SickKids Staff. "Social and Emotional Development of Babies." AboutKidsHealth, 21 Sept. 9AD, https://www.aboutkidshealth.ca/Article?-contentid=487&language=English#:~:text=Up%20to%20about%20 eight%20months,is%20deliberately%20thwarting%20their%20goal.

2　Singer, Michael. The Untethered Soul: The Journey Beyond Yourself. New Harbinger Publications, 2013.

3　Maslow, Abraham. "Classics in the History of Psychology -- A. H. Maslow (1943) a Theory of Human Motivation." Classics in the History of Psychology, Aug. 2000, psychclassics.yorku.ca/Maslow/motivation.htm.

4　Kondo, Marie, and Emily Woo Zeller. The Life-Changing Magic of Tidying Up: The Japanese Art of Decluttering and Organizing. MP3-Unabridged CD ed., Tantor Audio, 2015.

5　Sagiv, L., Roccas, S., Cieciuch, J. et al. Personal values in human life. Nat Hum Behav 1, 630–639 (2017). https://doi.org/10.1038/s41562-017-0185-3

6　Covey, Stephen. The 7 Habits of Highly Effective People: Powerful Lessons in Personal Change. Simon and Schuster, 2013.

7　Gates, Bill. "Home | Bill Gates." Gatesnotes.Com, www.gatesnotes.com. Accessed 5 Apr. 2022.

8　Wenner, Melinda. "Study: Doing Good Makes You Feel Good." Livescience.Com, Future US, Inc., 4 May 2007, www.livescience.com/4443-study-good-feel-good.html.

9　"Loneliness and Social Isolation Linked to Serious Health Conditions." CDC - Centers for Disease and Control and Prevention, www.cdc.gov/aging/publications/features/lonely-older-adults.html#:%7E:text=Health%20Risks%20of%20Loneliness&text=Recent%20studies%20found%20that%3A,percent%20increased%20risk%20of%20dementia. Accessed 25 Mar. 2022.

10　Leonard, Jayne. "What Are the Effects of Solitary Confinement on Health?" Medical News Today, 7 Aug. 2020, www.medicalnewstoday.com/articles/solitary-confinement-effects#mental-health-effects.

11　Wolters, Eugene. "Our Language Shapes Our Reality, New Study Suggests." Critical-Theory, 15 Aug. 2013, www.critical-theory.com/language-shapes-reality-study-reveals/#:%7E:text=Our%20Language%20Shapes%20Our%20Reality%2C%20New%20Study%20Suggests&text=Verbal%20cues%20may%20actively%20shape,reality%2C%20a%20 new%20study%20shows.&text=That%20our%20language%20actively%20 shapes,which%20exists%20independent%20of%20language.

Made in the USA
Middletown, DE
13 March 2024